mumford/25,00

Date Due

BRODART Cat. No. 23 233 Printed in U.S.A

VIKING REPRINT EDITIONS

GOVERNMENT BY INVESTIGATION

ALAN BARTH

Government by Investigation

Monarchical institutions have thrown an odium upon despotism; let us beware lest democratic republics should restore oppression, and should render it less odious and less degrading in the eyes of the many, by making it still more onerous to the few.

—ALEXIS DE TOCQUEVILLE

AUGUSTUS M. KELLEY • PUBLISHERS

CLIFTON 1973

First Published 1955

(New York: The Viking Press, Inc.)

Copyright 1955 by Alan Barth

RE-ISSUED 1973 BY

AUGUSTUS M. KELLEY · PUBLISHERS

Clifton New Jersey 07012

By Arrangement with THE VIKING PRESS

Library of Congress Cataloging in Publication Data

Barth, Alan.
  Government by investigation.

  (Viking reprint editions)
  Reprint of the ed. published by Viking Press,
New York.
  1. Governmental ivestigations--United States.
I. Title.
₍JK1123.A2B3 1973₎   328'.34   71-122068
ISBN 0-678-03150-9

PRINTED IN THE UNITED STATES OF AMERICA
by SENTRY PRESS, NEW YORK, N. Y. 10013

For

Gene and Florine

CONTENTS

GOVERNMENT BY INVESTIGATION

CHAPTER I

A BALANCE OF POWERS

A legislative, an executive, and a judicial power comprehend the whole of what is meant and understood by government. It is by balancing each of these powers against the other two, that the efforts in human nature towards tyranny can alone be checked and restrained, and any freedom preserved in the Constitution.[1]

I

POLITICAL liberty consists of limitations upon the authority of governments. It is in the nature of power to expand and to seek its own aggrandizement. Through a variety of rationalizations—in the name of efficiency or economy, in the name of the public welfare, in the name of national security—power presses always at the boundaries prescribed for it and can be held within these boundaries only by countervailing power.

It was an understanding of this fundamental political fact that constituted the genius of the American Constitutional Convention of 1787. The doctrine that government should comprise three distinct and counterbalancing elements did not originate with that convention. It was enunciated by Aristotle in ancient Athens, reshaped by John Locke, embellished by Montesquieu, and by the time of the American Revolution had become axiomatic among the libertarian political thinkers of the eighteenth century. Seek-

[1] John Adams, letter to Richard Henry Lee, November 15, 1775; quoted by Benjamin F. Wright, "The Federalist on the Nature of Political Man," *Ethics*, January 1949, p. 9.

ing to establish a limited government, the Constitutional Convention of 1787 turned naturally to separation of powers as the means of making the limitation effective.

"The doctrine of the separation of powers was adopted by the Convention of 1787," Justice Brandeis once observed, "not to promote efficiency but to preclude the exercise of arbitrary power." [2] This cornerstone of the governmental edifice erected by the Constitutional Convention was meant to assure a structure which would be sheltering but not confining. It was designed to support a government as strong as it needed to be to carry on its designated and limited functions, yet not so strong as to become oppressive.

Concentration of power was considered the very fountainhead of oppression. This was a doctrine so generally recognized that a considerable portion of *The Federalist* was devoted to assuring and reassuring the public that the Constitutional Convention had been fully on guard against this danger and had taken the fullest possible measures to avert it. Madison was enunciating no more than a truism of the times when he said, "The accumulation of all powers, legislative, executive, and judiciary, in the same hands, whether of one, a few, or many, and whether hereditary, self-appointed, or elective, may justly be pronounced the very definition of tyranny." [3] About this, no educated men of that period had any disposition to argue. The question was whether the Constitution adequately safeguarded the new nation against such an accumulation of powers.

Separation by itself was not enough. The members of the convention were aware that power can be contained only by power; and so they sought to create not merely separation but a balance of forces, each of which would operate to hold the others in check. As John Adams observed in the quotation at the head of this chapter, it is only *"by balancing each of these powers against the other two"* that any freedom can be preserved.

The separated powers of the United States government are

[2] *Myers* v. *United States,* 272 U.S. 52 (1926).
[3] *The Federalist,* No. XLVII (1778).

now gravely out of balance. It is the purpose of this book to show that the legislative branch has acquired a dominance which is becoming a peril to liberty. The imbalance has been brought about in large measure through an old and necessary instrument of legislative action which lately has got altogether out of hand —the congressional investigating committee. Congress has, increasingly during the past decade, ominously during the past five years, used its indispensable investigating power in ways that encroach upon the jurisdiction of the executive branch of the government; it has used this power in ways that usurp and corrupt the special functions of the judicial branch; and, most dangerous of all, it has used this power in ways that extend the authority of the government into vital areas of American life traditionally reserved for private—that is to say, non-governmental—control.

This growth of legislative domination is not peculiar to the United States. It occurs from time to time in every representative government. Legislatures tend always to be expansionist. Only the most vigorous and forceful countervailing power can contain them. Walter Lippmann has noted this tendency in virtually all the free governments of the present day:

> As we can see only too well in Washington, it is in the world today no easy matter to bring into being sufficiently strong governments by the process of popular election. There are, of course, special circumstances in each country. But there is also a common and fundamental condition in the constitutional disorder of the Western world. It is one well known to the founding fathers of the American republic and one which was their constant preoccupation. It is that the legislative assemblies, being closest to the voters, are exerting their power to invade and to usurp the prerogatives of the Executive. Since it is impossible for assemblies to govern a country, they exercise their usurped power by preventing the Executive from governing it.[4]

The danger of legislative supremacy was indeed, as Mr. Lippmann observes, a "constant preoccupation" of the fathers of the American Republic. The pages of *The Federalist* and the records of the Constitutional Convention of 1787 are filled with expres-

[4] Walter Lippmann, "Today and Tomorrow," *New York Herald Tribune,* June 21, 1953.

sions of anxiety about this imbalance. Those who drafted the Constitution did all they could to build dikes that would hold the tides of congressional ambition and aggression within safe boundaries. Recognizing at the same time, however, the need for flexibility in the Constitution, they knew that the real reliance for the containment of Congress must rest upon the countervailing powers of the executive and the judicial branches of the government. Accordingly, they contrived to allow these powers the fullest possible expression.

But if a balance of powers is to be maintained, then each of the branches of the government must guard its prerogatives jealously and assert power in order to keep the power of the others within its proper sphere. Each must refrain from any relinquishment of its rights and its authority. Each must defend itself resolutely from invasion by the others. Only strong Presidents and strong judges can cope with strong congresses.

II

Naturally enough it was upon executive power that eighteenth-century Americans tended to look with the deepest suspicion. They had had intimate and painful experience of despotism on the part of the colonial governors, who were George III's delegated executives in the new world. In the main, the colonists had been obliged to look to the colonial legislatures for representation of their interests and championship of their rights. And so, understandably, they were disposed to be more suspicious of executive than of legislative authority. Most of the early state constitutions exalted the legislature at the expense of the executive branch.

This was true to so great an extent that Madison felt constrained to point out in *The Federalist* that the founders of the several state governments which were to join in the formation of the American Republic

. . . seem never for a moment to have turned their eyes from the danger to liberty from the over-grown and over-grasping prerogatives of an hereditary magistrate, supported and fortified by an hereditary branch of the legislative authority. They seem never to have recollected the danger from legislative usurpers, which, by assembling of power in the same hands, must lead to the same tyranny as is threatened by executive usurpations.[5]

Madison went so far, indeed, as to declare that "it is against the enterprising ambition of this department [the legislative] that the people ought to indulge all their jealousy and exhaust all their precautions.[6] And he proceeded to quote the warning expressed by Jefferson in his *Notes on the State of Virginia*—a warning which today seems wonderfully foresighted:

All the powers of government, legislative, executive, and judiciary, result to the legislative body. The concentrating these in the same hands, is precisely the definition of despotic government. It will be no alleviation, that these powers will be exercised by a plurality of hands, and not by a single one. One hundred and seventy-three despots would surely be as oppressive as one.[7]

That the legislature had despotic potentialities and needed to be kept within appropriate bounds by countervailing power was voiced explicitly at the Constitutional Convention by Gouverneur Morris:

One great object of the Executive is to control the Legislature. The Legislature will continually seek to aggrandize those critical moments produced by war, invasion or convulsion for that purpose. It is necessary then that the Executive Magistrate should be the guardian of the people, even of the lower classes, agst Legislative tyranny, against the Great & the wealthy who in the course of things will necessarily compose the Legislative body.[8]

There is abundant evidence, in short, to support Professor Binkley's observation that "where the makers of the state constitutions had feared and subdued the Executive, the dominant element in the Philadelphia Convention was deeply concerned

[5] *The Federalist,* No. XLVIII (1778).
[6] Ibid., p. 340.
[7] Ibid., p. 341.
[8] Max Farrand, *Records of the Federal Convention* (New Haven: Yale University Press, 1911), Vol. II, pp. 52–54.

lest the popular organ, the Congress, should play the tyrant.
. . . Among the delegates there developed a pronounced consensus that the national legislature would have to be decisively
checked." [9]

This determination to check the legislature was expressed in
an extremely elastic definition of executive authority as compared
with a precisely limited assignment of powers to Congress. Article I—beginning, "All legislative Powers *herein granted* shall
be vested in a Congress of the United States"—imposes a limitation very different from the sweeping grant of Article II, which
states: "The executive Power shall be vested in a President of the
United States of America."

The convention, moreover, abandoned proposals that the President be chosen by the legislature and that he be guided by an
executive council. Instead it contrived ways to make him independent of the legislative branch. His office, along with that of
the Vice-President, is the only office in the United States which
has the whole American people as its constituency. The President is therefore uniquely the representative of the entire public
and derives from this special status a powerful popular support.
He was intended to be something much more than a mere executor of laws enacted by Congress. "It seems to have been no accident, on the part of those who gave the Constitution its phrasing,"
says Professor Binkley, "that the President's oath was made to
read that he 'execute the office' of President, not merely enforce
the law." [10] A large measure of initiative and of countervailing
power in relation to the legislature was assigned to him.

How well has this assignment served to keep the power of
the legislative branch within the balanced bounds drawn by the
men who framed the Constitution? The answer depends upon the
character of the particular President in office. Under a strong
President, this countervailing power has been effectively exer-

[9] Wilfred E. Binkley, *President and Congress* (New York: Alfred A. Knopf,
1947), p. 21.
[10] Ibid., p. 24.

cised—so effectively, indeed, as sometimes to justify concern over executive supremacy. Under less energetic executives, Congress has established an overwhelming dominance; and this would seem to have become more nearly the rule than the exception.

"In ordinary times," said Woodrow Wilson, "it is not from the Executive that the most dangerous encroachments are to be apprehended. The legislature is the aggressive spirit." [11] And it seemed to him when he published his extraordinarily discerning analysis, *Congressional Government,* in 1885 that "the noble charter of fundamental law given us by the Convention of 1787 is still our Constitution; but it is now our *form of government* rather in name than in reality, the form of the Constitution being one of nicely adjusted, ideal balances, whilst the actual form of our present government is simply a scheme of congressional supremacy. . . ." [12]

This judgment was based, no doubt, on the experience of the two decades following the Civil War. But it must have undergone almost immediate modification during the administration of Grover Cleveland, which began in the very year that *Congressional Government* was published. It must have been modified still more by Theodore Roosevelt's use of presidential power and, of course, by Wilson's own forceful leadership of Congress as long as it remained under the control of his party. The presidency of Franklin Roosevelt would have afforded him yet another illustration of what can be done by a powerful President. But if these cases would have made him qualify his generalization, it is by no means clear that he would have had to reverse it or to discard it; indeed, they show simply that resolute and resourceful individuals can offset the natural domination of the legislative branch and keep the system in equilibrium. The system is like a tricycle, with the presidency serving as the lead wheel. It is bound to go askew unless that wheel directs its course.

[11] Woodrow Wilson, *Congressional Government* (Boston: Houghton, Mifflin & Co., 14th Impression, 1900), pp. 36–37.
[12] Ibid., p. 6.

III

So far as the judiciary is concerned, much less was expected of it as a wielder of countervailing power. "The judiciary," said Alexander Hamilton, "is beyond comparison the weakest of the three departments of power." [13]

Nevertheless Hamilton expressed plainly what was the common sense of the time and what was considered indisputable by the members of the Constitutional Convention: that "there is no liberty, if the power of judging be not separated from the legislative and executive powers." Thus the convention sought to establish an independent judiciary by giving its judges life tenure during good behavior, forbidding a diminution of their compensation during their continuance in office, and providing, at least by implication, that the Supreme Court should have power to declare any act of Congress invalid. The Constitution's restraints on the legislature, Hamilton declared, "can be preserved in practice no other way than through the medium of courts of justice, whose duty it must be to declare all acts contrary to the manifest tenor of the Constitution void. Without this, all the reservations of particular rights or privileges would amount to nothing." [14]

This authority to invalidate acts of Congress, first asserted by John Marshall, became, of course, a source of bitter frustration in the long period when the Supreme Court arrogated to itself the powers of a super-legislature and forbade both the federal government and the states to take effective action toward the solution of pressing economic and social problems. Nevertheless it is an authority in the absence of which the Supreme Court would have been feeble indeed and the legislature might well have reduced the Constitution to a mere form of words. If judicial review has sometimes seemed to give the Supreme Court a tyrannical power, it has, on the whole, served to keep tyranny in check. And the independence of the judiciary has contributed more than any

[13] *The Federalist*, No. LXXVIII (1778).
[14] Ibid.

other factor to the boast of Americans that theirs is a government of laws, not of men. The courts, on the whole, have been, as Hamilton said they were designed to be, "an intermediate body between the people and the legislature, in order, among other things, to keep the latter within the limits assigned to their authority." [15]

IV

This book will attempt, first, an examination of legislative trespassing upon executive authority; second, of legislative intrusion upon the independence of the judiciary; third, of legislative invasion of those rights and powers reserved, under the Ninth and Tenth articles of the Bill of Rights, to the people of the United States.

In a sense, it is not so much Congress itself as certain agencies of Congress—its investigating committees—that have been responsible for this usurpation. These committees have seized powers far beyond the authority delegated to them by the Senate or the House of Representatives. They have become roving satrapies unrestrained by their parent bodies and thrusting themselves, under the guise of investigation, into every kind of public and private business. In the absence of any responsible control by Congress, they have taken on a life of their own and a force of their own. This tendency was noted bitterly by Fisher Ames long ago. From his seat as a member of the 4th Congress, he wrote to Hamilton:

The efficiency of the government is reduced to its minimum, the proneness of the popular body to usurpation is already advancing to its maximum. Committees are already the ministers; and while the House indulges in jealousy of encroachments in its functions, which are properly deliberative, it does not perceive they are impaired and nullified by the monopoly as well as the perversion of information by the committees.[16]

[15] Ibid.
[16] Alexander Hamilton, *Works* (1851), Vol. IV, p. 201; quoted by Binkley, op. cit., p. 40.

The committees, particularly those empowered to investigate subversion, have sometimes managed, in effect, to control administration by threatening to subject executive officials to public disgrace if they resist efforts to dictate their programs and select their personnel. Committees have sometimes conducted legislative trials, summoning citizens before them and condemning them by proceedings that ignore the fundamental rights guaranteed in courts of law. And they have sometimes conducted censorial inquiries into the administration of universities, churches, newspapers, and philanthropic foundations—areas where Congress has no jurisdiction at all. In short, the power of Congress to investigate—an indispensable and salutary power—is being perverted today in ways that threaten to upset the balance of the American constitutional system and to institute a legislative dictatorship.

Dictatorship need not take the form of an individual on horseback. It may come about quite as disastrously, quite as oppressively, through legislative domination. Jefferson's observation that "one hundred and seventy-three despots would surely be as oppressive as one" reflects an unassailable political insight. Indeed, dictatorship by a plurality of hands, if it ever develops, is likely to be at once more ferocious and more difficult to overcome than dictatorship by any single pair of hands. Just as the most ruthless form of violence is mob violence, the most ruthless form of tyranny is legislative tyranny. Rivalry among those who wield it impels them to outdo one another in excesses. And precisely because they are without individual responsibility, they are likely to give way to the most reckless collective irresponsibility.

This is the peril which the authors of the Constitution foresaw and against which they tried to guard. The safeguard against it lies in the Constitution itself—in the restoration of a balance of powers through the reassertion of countervailing power—and in self-restraint and an acceptance of responsibility on the part of Congress. These are the inescapable conditions of democratic government.

CHAPTER II

THE INVESTIGATING POWER

It is the proper duty of a representative body to look diligently into every affair of government and to talk much about what it sees. It is meant to be the eyes and the voice, and to embody the wisdom and will of its constituents. Unless Congress have and use every means of acquainting itself with the acts and the disposition of the administrative agents of the government, the country must be helpless to learn how it is being served; and unless Congress both scrutinize these things and sift them by every form of discussion, the country must remain in embarrassing, crippling ignorance of the very affairs which it is most important that it should understand and direct. The informing function of Congress should be preferred even to its legislative function. The argument is not only that discussed and interrogated administration is the only pure and efficient administration, but, more than that, that the only really self-governing people is that people which discusses and interrogates its administration.[1]

I

THE POWER to investigate is coeval with the power to legislate and indispensable to it. It serves the legislature in two vital ways: (1) as a direct aid to legislation; (2) as a brake upon the power of the executive branch.

Congress first asserted an investigating power as long ago as 1792. The House of Representatives in that early year of the

[1] Wilson, op. cit., p. 303.

Republic created a select committee, with subpoena powers, to find out why an expedition of American troops under General St. Clair had been ignominiously routed by Indians. Power to conduct such an inquiry was held to be implicit in the power to authorize armies and to appropriate funds for their maintenance. The power has never been seriously questioned since that time.

Neither has its utility been questioned by any serious student of American government. Since the time of its inquiry into General St. Clair's disaster, Congress has authorized and conducted close to a thousand special investigations—more than half of them during the last quarter of a century. Some of these have been frivolous and some have served only the interest of headline-hunters. Some have undoubtedly produced real mischief. Some have amounted to outright attempts by the legislature to usurp executive functions—for instance, when Radical Republican congressmen in 1862 adopted a resolution to investigate the Union defeats at Bull Run and Ball's Bluff and established a Joint Committee on the Conduct of the War; it exposed military errors and inefficiencies, but it also tried to take over from the generals and the President the actual conduct of military affairs. Some undertook legislative trials, egregiously invading the domain of the judiciary. Some trespassed grievously on the rights of individuals.

But if congressional use of the power to investigate produced occasional excesses, it also produced tremendous boons to the democratic process. Through it, Congress effected valuable reforms in American life and imposed a salutary check on the executive branch of the government. It would be as foolish, indeed, to condemn the investigating power because it is now and then abused as to condemn, say, the principle of freedom of the press because some newspapers sometimes behave irresponsibly. The proper limits of the investigating power are difficult to define—and still more difficult to enforce. But the power is nevertheless invaluable.

The utility of the investigating power as a direct aid and adjunct to the business of legislating seems self-evident. Calling it "perhaps the most necessary of all the powers underlying the legislative function," Senator J. William Fulbright of Arkansas declared that "the power to investigate provides the legislature with eyes and ears and a thinking mechanism."[2] Since the function of law is to correct inequities and to control antisocial tendencies, Congress could scarcely legislate at all without first obtaining knowledge of the conditions it aimed to correct and control. The delegation of a power of inquiry to standing or special committees seems the obvious if not the only way in which such knowledge can be obtained by a large legislative assembly. This kind of inquiry, moreover, enables diverse individuals and groups to submit their views to Congress.

It would be easy to cite a long list of special-committee investigations—apart from the day-to-day hearings of standing committees—which produced information immensely helpful to Congress as preparation for the work of lawmaking itself. One exemplary illustration is the study of the life-insurance industry conducted by Charles Evans Hughes, as counsel for a special committee of the Senate in 1905. It brought to light serious shortcomings in the regulation of life-insurance companies and pointed the way toward needed remedial legislation. The revelation of this need could hardly have been brought about as effectively by any other device. The investigation of public utilities by the Black Committee in 1935 similarly led to legislation regulating public-utility holding companies.

The second service rendered by the investigating power—its usefulness as a brake upon the power of the executive branch —is at least equally important. It furnishes a lever with which the legislature exerts its countervailing power against the Executive. Control over appropriations would lose much of its meaning if it were not accompanied by an authority to scrutinize the uses to which appropriations had been put; the lawmaking prerogative would be a nearly empty one if it did not also imply a right to

[2] J. William Fulbright, "Congressional Investigations: Significance for the Legislative Process," *University of Chicago Law Review*, Vol. 18, No. 3 (Spring 1951), p. 441.

call the Executive to account for the administration of the laws. Inseparable from the power to legislate is the power to inquire into the efficacy of legislation and the efficiency with which it has been carried into effect.

So much of governing lies outside the range of legislation, moreover—so much of it is determined by the initiative of the President in foreign affairs, by the executive power to issue regulations and formulate methods for the execution of congressional mandates—that Congress would be hopelessly subordinated if it did not possess the power to check the Executive through investigation. It is this device more than any other which prevents misconduct in the executive branch and keeps executive authority within the limits set for it.

"Instead of the function of governing, for which it is radically unfit," John Stuart Mill observed, "the proper office of a representative assembly is to watch and control the government: to throw the light of publicity on its acts: to compel a full exposition and justification of all of them which any one considers questionable; to censure them if found condemnable, and, if the men who compose the government abuse their trust, or fulfill it in a manner which conflicts with the deliberate sense of the nation, to expel them from office, and either expressly or virtually appoint their successors." [3]

The investigations conducted by Senators Thomas J. Walsh and Burton K. Wheeler of Montana in the 1920s, which revealed the corruption and misconduct in the Harding administration, are obvious cases in point. Other examples, from the present as well as from the past, can be cited in abundance—the discovery, for instance, of laxities in the Reconstruction Finance Corporation and of outright graft in the Internal Revenue Service during the Truman administration. Such discoveries serve admirably to counteract executive abuses. And beyond their immediate effect, of course, lies the restraining influence constantly exerted by the threat that Congress may turn an investigative searchlight upon any executive agency.

[3] John Stuart Mill, *Representative Government*, Everyman Edition, p. 239.

The investigating power has given rise, especially in recent years, to abuses of the gravest order—abuses which threaten to make the power destructive and despotic. But the need is to curb the abuses without curbing the power itself. For any essential impairment of the power to investigate would result inevitably in an impairment of the American constitutional system.

II

Though the authority of Congress to investigate is unchallengeable, the scope of that authority has been challenged, and on numerous occasions—in political terms by the executive branch of the government and in the courts by private citizens. So far as the conflict between the executive and legislative branches of the government is concerned, the courts have quite understandably regarded this as political in character and therefore not susceptible of adjudication by the judicial branch. The courts have had a good deal to say, however—and much that is contradictory—about the rights of citizens in regard to congressional inquiries.

The power of investigation would be a dubious one if it did not embrace power to summon witnesses and to compel testimony from those that proved reluctant or recalcitrant. This power was assumed by Congress from the outset and was frequently asserted, for nearly a century, without any serious opposition, either in or out of Congress. On a number of occasions witnesses charged with contempt of Congress for refusing to answer questions put to them by investigating committees were haled before the bar of the Senate or the House and directly sentenced to imprisonment or fines by those bodies, under their inherent powers. It was a punishment for contempt inflicted in just this way that brought about the first significant judicial check on the congressional power of investigation in 1881.

A special committee of the House had been set up to look into the operations of a real-estate pool involved in the Jay Cooke bankruptcy. Substantial government funds had been deposited with the bankrupt company. Hallet Kilbourn, the manager of the pool, refused to produce certain papers demanded by the committee, or to identify men who were associated with him in the venture. The House declared him in contempt and ordered him confined "in the common jail of the District of Columbia" until he should be ready to answer the committee's questions. Kilbourn was released on a writ of habeas corpus, and the Supreme Court subsequently declared his confinement beyond the proper power of Congress.

The opinion of the court, written by Justice Miller, was sweeping in its condemnation of Congress and attempted to prescribe extremely narrow and rigid limits for congressional investigation. The court attacked the investigation on three grounds: that the resolution establishing the committee was outrageously vague; that the House of Representatives had no authority to inquire into matters not directly pertinent to pending or contemplated legislation; and that the House, in punishing Kilbourn, had "assumed a power which could only be properly exercised by another branch of the government because the power was in its nature clearly judicial." Justice Miller's indignation still crackles through his opinion after the passage of seventy-odd years:

We are sure that no person can be punished for contumacy as a witness before either House, unless his testimony is required in a matter into which that House has jurisdiction to inquire, and we feel equally sure that neither of these bodies possesses the general power of making inquiry into the private affairs of the citizen.[4]

The Kilbourn case was the only occasion until 1953 on which the Supreme Court declared a particular congressional inquiry to be improper. Perhaps the court's subsequent self-restraint was attributable in part to the ineffectuality of the restraint it had endeavored to impose. Although the Kilbourn decision cast a heavy shadow on the investigating power for nearly half a century, both Houses of Congress zealously continued to pursue investigations.

[4] *Kilbourn* v. *Thompson*, 103 U.S. 168 (1881).

The Supreme Court has never explicitly overruled *Kilbourn* v. *Thompson,* but it has swept around it with the curious kind of end run it resorts to when it wants to avoid plunging directly into a solid line of its own creation. It did not reverse the principles enunciated, but it significantly changed the emphasis put upon them. It returned to the issue in a remarkably similar case in 1927.

A Senate select committee investigating the administration of the Department of Justice under Harry Daugherty subpoenaed the former Attorney General's brother, Mally S. Daugherty, as a witness. When Mally Daugherty failed to appear, or even to acknowledge the subpoena, a deputy sergeant-at-arms of the Senate, John J. McGrain, arrested him. He was released, however, by a writ of habeas corpus and appealed to the courts on the basis of the Kilbourn decision. It took the Supreme Court three years to make up its mind—the case was argued in 1924 and not decided until 1927—but when it did so, it held squarely that Congress has the power at least to investigate and to require testimony essential to its work of lawmaking. Justice Willis Van Devanter said for a unanimous court:

We are of opinion that the power of inquiry—with process to enforce it—is an essential and appropriate auxiliary to the legislative function. . . .

A legislative body cannot legislate wisely or effectively in the absence of information respecting the conditions which the legislation is intended to affect or change; and where the legislative body does not itself possess the requisite information—which not infrequently is true —recourse must be had to others who do possess it.[5]

The court left no room for doubt as to congressional authority to require witnesses to respond to proper and pertinent questions. Either House of Congress, it declared,

. . . has power, through its own processes, to compel a private individual to appear before it or one of its committees and give testimony needed to enable it efficiently to exercise a legislative function belong-

[5] *McGrain* v. *Daugherty,* 273 U.S. 135, 174–75 (1927).

ing to it under the Constitution. . . . The power is so far incidental to the legislative function as to be implied.[6]

The court paid homage to its past, however, to the extent of reasserting that the investigating power is not plenary and can be exercised only within bounds of pertinency and without invading areas of privacy reserved by the Constitution. "A witness," said the court, "rightfully may refuse to answer where the bounds of the power are exceeded or the questions are not pertinent to the matter under inquiry."

What constitutes privacy upon which Congress may not trespass remains uncertain, although judicial construction of the standard now seems as excessively loose as it was once excessively rigid. The issue has been posed sharply in recent years in connection with questions regarding membership in the Communist party and adherence to Communist doctrines. Witnesses who stood upon the First Amendment to the Constitution as a ground for refusing to answer questions regarding political beliefs and affiliations—maintaining that the right to speak freely necessarily implied a right to remain silent about matters of opinion—found it to be a quicksand.

Although the Supreme Court has not spoken on the point, two Circuit Courts of Appeals have held—in each case with a vigorous dissenting opinion—that a committee of Congress may inquire into belief and affiliation in order to determine whether these find expression in propaganda or other activities that create a clear and present danger which Congress may wish to prevent through legislation. The Court of Appeals for the District of Columbia, acknowledging that such inquiry trenches upon the area protected by the First Amendment, said in its decision upholding the conviction of Dr. Edward K. Barsky for contempt of Congress:

If Congress has power to inquire into the subjects of communism and the Communist party, it has power to identify the individuals who believe in communism and those who belong to the party. The nature and

6 Ibid., p. 176.

scope of the program and activities depend in large measure upon the character and number of their adherents. . . . In our view, it would be sheer folly as a matter of governmental policy for an existing government to refrain from inquiry into potential threats to its existence or security until danger was clear and present. And for the judicial branch of government to hold the legislative branch to be without power to make such inquiry until the danger is clear and present, would be absurd. How, except upon inquiry, would the Congress know whether the danger is clear and present? There is a vast difference between the necessities for inquiry and the necessities for action. The latter may be only when danger is clear and present, but the former is when danger is reasonably represented as potential.[7]

In a distinguished dissent, Judge Henry W. Edgerton furnished what is likely to stand as the most cogent and comprehensive case against the House Committee on Un-American Activities. "The investigation," he said, "restricts the freedom of speech by uncovering and advertising expressions of unpopular views." Moreover, as he saw it, this restriction was its purpose; it aimed not at the discovery of information for the guidance of Congress in fashioning legislation but at the exposure of individuals for the sake of punishing them by publicity. And this punishment, in his view, operates as a strong deterrent to free expression.

"The committee and its members," Judge Edgerton went on, "have repeatedly said in terms or in effect that its main purpose is to do by exposure and publicity what it believes may not validly be done by legislation. This is as much as to say that its purpose is to punish or burden propaganda. . . . What Congress may not restrain, Congress may not restrain by exposure and publicity."

And, finally, Judge Edgerton offered a specific rejoinder to the rhetorical question posed by Judge E. Barrett Prettyman in the opinion of the court:

The court asks, "How, except upon inquiry, would the Congress know whether the danger is clear and present?" The context shows that this means, "How, except upon *congressional* inquiry . . . ?" The

[7] 167 F. 2nd 241, 246–47 (1948).

answer is: through the Department of Justice, whose duty it is, if clear and present danger can be discovered, to enforce the law of 1940, which makes it a crime to advocate overthrow of the government by force; through the intelligence services; and through any new agency that Congress may think it useful to create. As the House Committee's history shows, no dangerous propaganda that eludes other agencies is likely to be discovered by a congressional inquiry. But a congressional inquiry, however superfluous, to discover whether there is a clear and present danger, could be authorized and could be conducted without violating the First Amendment. The premise that the government must have power to protect itself by discovering whether it is in clear and present danger of overthrow by violence is sound. But it does not support the conclusion that Congress may compel men to disclose their personal opinions, to a committee and also to the world, on topics ranging from communism, however remotely and peaceably achieved, to the "American system of checks and balances," the British Empire, and the Franco government of Spain. . . .

The free speech point comes to this. Congressional action that is either intended or likely to restrict expression of opinion that Congress may not prohibit violates the First Amendment. Congressional action in the nature of investigation is no exception. Civil liberties may not be abridged in order to determine whether they should be abridged.

Judge Edgerton surely put his scalpel upon the center of this aching issue. The real violation of liberty arises from the purpose of the Un-American Activities Committee to do by exposure and publicity what may not be done by legislation—that is, to punish men for associations and beliefs. There has arisen in Congress a view that the investigating power embraces a general informing function—distinct from the function of obtaining information needed for lawmaking and from the function of supervising and checking the executive branch. According to this view, the investigating power may properly be used simply to inform the people about emergent problems. But no court has ever said that such a power exists.

"Sometimes," Senator Fulbright observed, "the congressional investigation results only in public disclosure—or exposure. When this is the case, the results may be regarded as an appeal to public opinion, an invitation to the people to say whether or not they discern the need for legislation which the legislators themselves have not yet seen fit to enact." [8]

No one can doubt that investigation may properly have this result—provided that it is concerned with an area in which Congress may legitimately contemplate legislation, and provided also that it is aimed at the "exposure" of a problem, not at the "exposure" of individual wrongdoing, a province of the courts. The purpose of inquiry is information, not punishment.

The view that investigating committees may undertake a generalized program of exposure for the sake of informing the public sometimes appeals for authority to Woodrow Wilson's observation about the informing function of Congress quoted at the head of this chapter. It should be noted, however, that Wilson was writing not about investigating committees but about discussion and interrogation within the main bodies of Congress. Moreover, he was writing specifically about legislative supervision of executive operations. There is certainly no warrant in what Wilson wrote for use of the investigating power to accomplish what Judge Edgerton condemned—exposure of the personal opinions of private citizens.

Congress does not need to expose individuals in order to expose the dimensions of the Communist problem. To compel men to confess beliefs and associations which will subject them to odium neither serves any legitimate congressional purpose nor comports with the American tradition of respect for privacy, heterodoxy, and conscience. This kind of investigation by an official governmental body can have no other purpose than to compel conformity, and no other consequence than to inhibit independence of thought and expression. The punishment of men for beliefs and associations must be no less repugnant to the Constitution of the United States when it is done by congressional investigation than when it is done by congressional legislation.

Perhaps, however, Professor Robert Carr of Dartmouth College, the most thorough student of the Un-American Activities Committee's record, was quite right in his melancholy observation

[8] Fulbright, op. cit., p. 443.

that "it seems wisest to abandon the hope that the Un-American Activities Committee may be curbed or even destroyed through judicial intervention." [9] Although there are numerous indications that the courts look with distaste, if not disgust, at the behavior of the Un-American Activities Committee and some other contemporary investigating bodies, the prevailing judicial view seems to be that expressed by Judge Prettyman in the Barsky case: "The remedy for unseemly conduct, if any, by committees of Congress is for Congress, or for the people; it is political and not judicial."

Justice Jackson, speaking for the Supreme Court, said much the same thing a year later: "I should not want to be understood as approving the use that the Committee on Un-American Activities has frequently made of its power. But I think it would be an unwarranted act of judicial usurpation to strip Congress of its investigatory power, or to assume for the courts the function of supervising congressional committees. I should . . . leave the responsibility for the behavior of its committees squarely on the shoulders of Congress." [10]

But if the courts are unwilling to "strip Congress of its investigatory power" or even to set any judicial limits upon the exercise of that power, perhaps they will police the power in a more modest way by seeing to it that individual committees do not arrogate power in ways not authorized by Congress. In this limited respect there may still be room for reliance on the courts. This, at any rate, is one basis of the appeal taken to the courts by two uncooperative witnesses in 1953—Harvey O'Connor and Corliss Lamont, who were summoned before Senator Joseph McCarthy's special investigating subcommittee of the Senate Committee on Government Operations and asked the customary questions about present or past membership in the Communist party. The occasion, or pretext, for calling them was that books they had written had been placed on the shelves of U.S. Information Service li-

[9] Robert K. Carr, *The House Committee on Un-American Activities* (Ithaca, N.Y.: Cornell University Press, 1952), pp. 449–50.
[10] *Eisler* v. *U.S.*, 338 U.S. 189, 196 (1949).

braries overseas. The two men sought no refuge in the Fifth Amendment's privilege against self-incrimination.

O'Connor was called before the McCarthy Subcommittee on July 14, 1953, and asked: "At the time you wrote the books which were purchased with taxpayers' money and put in our information libraries throughout the world, at that time were you a member of the Communist conspiracy?" O'Connor refused to answer the question on the following grounds:

Under the First Amendment to the Constitution, my writings, my books, and my political opinions are of no legitimate concern to this committee. If I have violated any laws in the writings that I have written, that is a proper concern for the law-enforcement agencies and not the proper concern of this committee. . . . My second point would be that this committee has no right to inquire into my writings, under the point of the constitutional limitations on the powers of Congress and its committees. . . . In the third place, I would object to the authority of the committee, under the statute by which it was created by Congress, to inquire into my writings or my political views.

Corliss Lamont, after pointing out that he was a private citizen not employed by the government in any fashion, stated: "To dispose of a question causing current apprehension, I am a loyal American and I am not now and never have been a member of the Communist party." Then, after reciting objections to the committee's questioning on a number of grounds, including the First Amendment and the separation of powers, he took specific objection to the committee's jurisdiction in these words:

The jurisdiction of this committee is further limited by the statutes which constitute and set forth its function and sphere of authority. Under the rules of the Senate and the statutes organizing the appointment of this Standing Committee, this committee has no authority to examine into the personal and private affairs of private citizens. Any action with regard to my books by officials of the government was done without my prior knowledge or consultation with me. I took no part in any proceedings involving any governmental authority and therefore this committee is without power to examine me under the rules and statutes governing it.

Since O'Connor and Lamont were not employed by the government in any way when Senator McCarthy's Subcommittee questioned them, it is hard to see how their personal opinions or political associations could be pertinent to any inquiry properly undertaken by a Committee on Government Operations or one of its subcommittees. And pertinency at least, the courts have held consistently, is a touchstone of validity in congressional inquiry. The language of the Legislative Reorganization Act defining the duties of the Committee on Government Operations is worth noting in this connection:

Such committee shall have the duty of—

(A) receiving and examining reports of the Comptroller General of the United States and of submitting such recommendations to the Senate as it deems necessary or desirable in connection with the subject matter of such reports;

(B) studying the operation of government activities at all levels with a view to determining its economy and efficiency;

(C) evaluating the effects of laws enacted to reorganize the legislative and executive branches of the government;

(D) studying intergovernmental relationships between the United States and the states and municipalities, and between the United States and international organizations of which the United States is a member.

It is one thing to strip Congress of its investigatory power and quite another to strip a committee of power which Congress never delegated to it. There would be no judicial usurpation in the latter form of judicial censure. The deference due Congress as a coordinate branch of the government is not due a committee or subcommittee spuriously acting in the name of Congress. And perhaps the courts, understandably wary of calling unconstitutional a resolution adopted by one of the Houses of Congress, will be more inclined to check a committee ranging beyond the jurisdiction assigned to it.

This was certainly the disposition of the courts in the Rumely case, decided by the United States Court of Appeals for the District of Columbia Circuit on April 29, 1952, and affirmed by the Supreme Court not quite a year later, on March 9, 1953. The case involved an investigation by a House of Representatives Select

Committee on Lobbying Activities—generally known as the Buchanan Committee—into the operation of the Federal Regulation of Lobbying Act.

Edward A. Rumely, secretary of an organization known as the Committee for Constitutional Government, which had registered under the terms of the Lobbying Act, was summoned before the Buchanan Committee and asked about the source of his organization's funds. The law required anyone receiving money to be used "directly or indirectly" to influence the course of legislation before Congress to report to the Clerk of the House of Representatives "the name and address of each person who has made a contribution of $500 or more." [11] It was discovered by the Buchanan Committee that shortly after the enactment of this law Rumely and his Committee for Constitutional Government had adopted a policy of rejecting and returning "contributions" in excess of $490; they asked the "contributors" instead to "purchase" books for distribution by the CCG, and it was candidly acknowledged by Rumely that this was done because they "didn't want to get into the position of reporting our contributors."

Rumely described the work of his organization in these terms: "Our lobbying consists of going out with a viewpoint to the country, and informing people and letting the people talk to their Members of the Congress." To this end, the CCG sometimes sent out half a million or more copies of a particular book. Rumely was ordered by the Buchanan Committee to submit the names of all purchasers of books or pamphlets. He declined. "I certainly refuse to disclose those names—not contemptuously, but respectfully," he said, "because I feel it is my duty to uphold the fundamental principles of the Bill of Rights. I think that there is no power to require of a publisher the names of the people who buy his products, and that you are exceeding your right." He pleaded also that the House of Representatives had not by its Resolution empowered the Buchanan Committee to make this demand upon him. He was cited for contempt of Congress and found guilty by a jury in a Federal District Court.

[11] 60 Stat. 839, 840; 2 U.S.C. (1946).

The Court of Appeals, dividing two to one, reversed the conviction. "It is our view," said Judge Prettyman, "that the Resolution of the House which created the Buchanan Committee and gave it power to investigate 'lobbying activities' did not confer the power which the government upon this appeal claims for it, relating to the identity of the purchasers of books from his company."

The premise on which this conclusion rested was that the House Resolution was intended "to mean lobbying in its commonly accepted sense, and did not purport to convey power to investigate efforts to influence public opinion." And Judge Prettyman added that "a serious constitutional question would arise if the House Resolution were to be interpreted to include the broad powers claimed for it by the committee." He left no doubt, moreover, as to his own view on this question: "If Congress had authorized its committee to inquire generally into attempts to influence public opinion upon national affairs by books, pamphlets, and other writing, its authorization would have been void." In a strongly argued dissent, Judge David L. Bazelon took a contrary view on both points.

The issue is as sharply focused here as in the Barsky case; and it is not easy to reconcile the two decisions by the same court. Judge Prettyman, who wrote the majority opinion in both cases, distinguished them on the ground that in the Barsky case "it was shown that the President and other responsible government officials had, with supporting evidentiary data, represented to the Congress that communism and the Communists are, in the current world situation, potential threats to the security of this country"—that they constituted, in other words, a clear and present danger justifying an admitted incursion into the area protected by the First Amendment. But it is hard to accept a mere executive—or even a legislative—declaration that a clear and present danger exists as justification for measures which would otherwise be invalid; determination of the existence of a clear and present danger is peculiarly a judicial function.

Judge Prettyman acknowledged forthrightly, in both the Barsky and Rumely cases, that "the public inquiry there involved was an impingement on free speech" and that "the realistic effect of public embarrassment is a powerful interference with the free expression of views." Perhaps, therefore, the essential test of the authority to inflict such embarrassment should be not the mere pertinence of the question to the subject of inquiry but the indispensability of the disclosure to a proper congressional purpose.

There are abundant indications that in both cases the purpose of exposing individual identities was not to inform either Congress or the country but to inflict precisely the kind of embarrassment that Judge Prettyman recognized as "a powerful interference with the free expression of views." In the Barsky case, indeed, the purpose was to subject a lawful political affiliation to punishment by publicity—in effect, to compel a registration not then required by law but subsequently made requisite by the McCarran Internal Security Act of 1950, the constitutionality of which has not yet been determined. In the Rumely case the committee's purpose appears, though less plainly, to have been to compel an identification of contributors already made requisite by the Regulation of Lobbying Act; a more appropriate way to do this would have been to let the Department of Justice prosecute Rumely and his CCG in a court of law for evasion of the Lobbying Act. The validity of the act could then have been judicially determined.

The Supreme Court reviewed the Rumely case—having refused to review the Barsky case and the earlier Josephson contempt-of-Congress case—and affirmed the Circuit Court unanimously, Justices Burton and Minton taking no part in the decision. Justice Frankfurter, speaking for a majority of the court, rested his opinion, as had Judge Prettyman, on the ground that Congress had not authorized the Buchanan Committee to inquire into indirect lobbying and that consequently the committee's demand for the identification of Rumely's supporters was unwarranted. He reached this conclusion, he said, in conformity with the doctrine that the court had an obligation, wherever possible, to construe acts of Congress in such a way as to avoid serious constitutional doubt.

The Rumely case was the first case since the Kilbourn decision in 1881 in which both appellate courts held that a committee of Congress had gone beyond its proper powers in trying to compel testimony before it. And, although the courts refrained from an attempt to delineate the boundaries of the investigating power, they reasserted that boundaries exist. Justice Douglas, in a concurring opinion in which he was joined by Justice Black, rejected the majority view that Congress intended the committee to investigate only direct lobbying and held the inquiry to be invalid on the constitutional ground that "inquiry into personal and private affairs is precluded. . . . And so is any matter in respect to which no valid legislation could be had."

The purpose of an inquiry seems the significant key to its validity. Questioning aimed at inhibiting expression or harassing nonconformity or conducting a legislative trial entails purposes that are unconstitutional. It is certainly possible to ban such questioning without impairing the ability of congressional committees to discharge their vitally important part of the legislative process. The right of Congress to inquire may, as Mr. Justice Holmes said of other rights, come into conflict with freedom of expression. The reconciliation of rights is the business of politics. In the conflict between the congressional investigating power and the rights of individuals, the aim must be to carry on the necessary functions of Congress with a minimum impairment of civil liberties.

A due regard for the importance of congressional investigations need not entail a total disregard for individual rights. To quote Judge Edgerton's Barsky dissent once more: "As the fact that some taxation is necessary does not validate everything done in the name of taxation, the fact that some investigation is necessary does not validate everything done in the name of investigation." To keep inquiry within proper bounds demands restraint. But all democratic government demands restraint and the accommodation of conflicting interests.

III

Presidents have been more successful than private citizens in resisting congressional inquiry they considered improper. From the time when George Washington declined to let the House of Representatives examine his correspondence with John Jay, nearly every President has felt obliged at some point to say "no" to the demands of an investigating body. And these refusals have been respected by Congress, although not without the bitterest remonstrances and recriminations on occasion.

The first issue between a President and a congressional investigating committee came in the case of the first President and the first investigation—the inquiry by a special House committee into the rout of General St. Clair's army by the Indians. The committee asked President Washington for the papers pertaining to the unfortunate episode; and after consultation with his Cabinet he acquiesced, observing that, although the House might institute inquiries and call for papers generally, "the Executive ought to communicate such papers as the public good would permit and ought to refuse those the disclosure of which would injure the public." [12] This rule has been followed by every succeeding President in the light of his individual judgment.

In recent years the exercise of executive discretion has been applied with a good deal of frequency to congressional committee requests for access to the confidential files and reports of the Federal Bureau of Investigation respecting individual government employees. President Franklin D. Roosevelt consistently refused to give these executive papers to Congress, despite frantic congressional insistence on a number of occasions that they be turned over to investigating bodies; but even during Mr. Roosevelt's administration the Department of Justice followed the practice of letting the Senate Judiciary Committee, or at least its chairman, see the FBI reports on persons nominated for federal

[12] Thomas Jefferson, *Writings* (1892), Vol. I, pp. 189–90, quoted by Binkley, op. cit., p. 41.

judgeships. In general, however, Mr. Roosevelt adhered firmly to the position that any public disclosure of these reports would be contrary to the public interest.

The considerations supporting this view are compelling. They were stated succinctly by the director of the FBI, J. Edgar Hoover, when he was resisting a demand from a Senate Foreign Relations subcommittee for confidential reports:

> The files do not consist of proved information alone. The files must be viewed as a whole. One report may allege crimes of a most despicable sort, and the truth or falsity of these charges may not emerge until several reports are studied, further investigations made, and the wheat separated from the chaff. Should a given file be disclosed, the issue would be far broader than concerns the subject of the investigation. Names of persons who by force of circumstance entered into the investigation might well be innocent of any wrong. To publicize their names without the explanation of their associations would be a grave injustice.

The confidential nature of FBI personnel reports was reasserted by President Truman. Indeed, he issued a formal directive to all officials and employees of the executive branch, forbidding them to accede to any congressional demand for loyalty files or reports without his express authority. On one or two occasions, however, Mr. Truman authorized a few members of Congress, under special circumstance, to examine abstracts of FBI reports—notably in connection with the investigation by a Senate Foreign Relations subcommittee in 1950 of Senator McCarthy's sensational charge that the State Department was rife with Communists.

The Eisenhower administration inherited the congressional clamor for FBI loyalty files in a peculiarly severe form, since the Republican members of Congress had insisted most vociferously that Mr. Truman must hand over to any committee of Congress anything it demanded. The first formidable test of the new administration's attitude came in connection with the bitter fight over the confirmation of Charles E. Bohlen, nominated by President Eisenhower to be ambassador to the Soviet Union.

The Constitution confers upon the Senate a coordinate power

with the President in the appointment of ambassadors, judges, and certain other officers of the United States. It makes such appointments dependent upon the Senate's advice and consent; but it does not vest in the Senate authority to initiate or to determine them. The role of the Senate was defined forcefully a long time ago by President Andrew Jackson:

The executive power vested in the Senate is neither that of "nominating" nor "appointing." It is merely a check upon the executive power of appointment. If individuals are proposed for appointment by the President by them deemed incompetent or unworthy, they may withhold their consent and the appointment cannot be made. They check the action of the Executive, but cannot in relation to those very subjects act themselves nor direct him. . . . The whole executive power being vested in the President, who is responsible for its exercise, it is a necessary consequence that he should have a right to employ agents of his own choice to aid him in the performance of his duties, and to discharge them when he is no longer willing to be responsible for their acts. In strict accordance with this principle, the power of removal, which, like that of appointment, is an original executive power, is left unchecked by the Constitution in relation to all executive officers, for whose conduct the President is responsible, while it is taken from him in relation to judicial officers, for whose acts he is not responsible.[13]

In the Bohlen confirmation fight there was a clear attempt by a body of senators to do something more than "check the action of the Executive." There was an apparent effort to direct him. For it became increasingly obvious that the objections to Bohlen were related neither to his character nor his competence, but rather to policy views imputed to him by reason of his association with the previous administration. The discretion commonly granted to the President in the selection of assistants has special pertinence in regard to the appointment of an ambassador, who is his personal representative abroad and for whose policy views he is directly responsible. Nominations to ambassadorships are rarely rejected by the Senate, and then only for some egregious want of fitness.

[13] Jackson's *Protest* to the Senate, April 15, 1834, quoted by Harold C. Syrett, *Andrew Jackson* (Indianapolis: Bobbs-Merrill Co., 1953), p. 233.

At the time of his nomination Bohlen was a Foreign Service officer of twenty-five years' experience, having joined the State Department during the Hoover administration in 1928. He was one of the few experienced American career diplomats with a thorough knowledge of the Russian language and of Russian culture and institutions. He had learned about communism at first hand by observing the Soviet purge trials when he was a junior member of the United States Embassy staff in Moscow. Because of his knowledge, he served as Russian-language interpreter for President Roosevelt at the Yalta Conference.

The Yalta Conference has come into a good deal of disfavor in recent years, at least among those disposed to look with disfavor upon all the works of Franklin Roosevelt. But Bohlen declined to acknowledge that there had been anything sinister or disloyal to the United States in the wartime President's talks with Premier Stalin and Prime Minister Churchill. Testifying before the Senate Foreign Relations Committee, which was to pass upon his nomination, Bohlen denied that the Yalta Agreement contributed to Soviet control of Poland and said simply that in his opinion the map of Europe would look very much as it does today even if there had been no Yalta pact. "I myself find it difficult to believe that these agreements were so favorable to Russia," he was quoted as having said at a closed hearing of the committee, "when Russia has found it in her interest to violate them openly and continuously. But the alternative was to ignore Eastern Europe. You could not afford not to make the attempt which was made at Yalta."

It was to be expected that this attitude would arouse, as it did, violent opposition from men who had for some years been seeking a revision of history that would have reversed the roles of Roosevelt and Hitler. Moreover, Bohlen had been counselor of the Department of State under Secretary Dean Acheson. McCarthy was explicit in making this a principal ground for his opposition to Bohlen. He called the American diplomat "one of Acheson's top lieutenants—not merely a servant but a policy-maker." The Senator recalled that he had "promised we'd clean out the Acheson crowd lock, stock, and barrel." And Senator Styles Bridges said that his objections were "based upon his [Bohlen's] identification and association with the Truman-Acheson-Bohlen policies which the people acted on last November."

After hearing an unequivocal endorsement of Bohlen by Secretary of State John Foster Dulles, the Foreign Relations Committee voted 15 to 0 to report his nomination favorably to the Senate. However, Senator Pat McCarran charged on the floor of the Senate that the security director of the State Department, R. W. Scott McLeod, found "he could not clear Mr. Bohlen on the basis of the FBI report" on him, and that McLeod had been "summarily overridden" by Secretary Dulles. To this, Dulles declared at a news conference later the same day that he had not overridden McLeod or even had any conflict with him. He added, moreover, that the security director had no authority to pass upon the fitness of a presidential nominee. Since there was derogatory information in the FBI report on Bohlen, McLeod had referred the responsibility of final decision to the Secretary.

For a time the objections to Bohlen arising from his identification with the Roosevelt-Truman foreign policy and with former Secretary of State Acheson were glossed over by reflections on him as a "security risk." The real nature of the opposition was revealed candidly, however, by Senator McCarthy in the course of the Senate debate on confirmation. Even if all security doubts about Bohlen were resolved, the Senator said, "I would still oppose his nomination, because I think we should not promote those in this administration who were part and parcel and heart of the Acheson disastrous, suicidal foreign-policy group." [14]

The debate provided the most comprehensive contemporary discussion of the right of a congressional committee or of Congress itself to demand FBI files. At the outset the chairman of the Foreign Relations Committee, Senator Alexander Wiley, said: "The Secretary of State has been very cooperative with the Foreign Relations Committee. . . . While Mr. Bohlen's nomination was being considered by the committee, Mr. Dulles offered to

[14] *Congressional Record,* March 23, 1953, p. 2274.

make available to the chairman the FBI summary. . . . The Secretary offered to give me this summary in order that I might evaluate the evidence. I had heard rumors, and I said to the Secretary, 'I should prefer that you evaluate the report.' " [15] Senator Wiley then quoted the Secretary's evaluation:

> There is no derogatory material whatsoever which questions the loyalty of Mr. Bohlen to the United States, or which suggests that he is not a good security risk, which suggests he is in any manner one who has leaked or been loose in his conversation or anything of that sort.[16]

Those opposed to confirmation pressed four demands: they asked that McLeod be called before the Foreign Relations Committee to testify on his evaluation of the FBI report; they asked that Secretary Dulles be recalled to testify under oath; Senator McCarthy alone suggested that Bohlen be given a "lie-detector" test; and dissemination of the FBI report was urged in varying degrees. These demands were overruled, in large measure through the prestige and power of the Senate Majority Leader, the late Senator Robert A. Taft. The proposal to put Dulles under oath he called "ridiculous"—a term he modified, when he revised his remarks for the *Congressional Record*, to read "an uncalled-for suggestion." And he added, "So far as I am concerned, Mr. Dulles' statement not under oath is just as good as Mr. Dulles' statement under oath." [17]

As for calling McLeod, Senator Taft said, "I should be very much opposed to such a course as that." It might lead to publication of the FBI file, which "would in a sense destroy the FBI. At least it might raise wholly unjustified questions as to the character of men in this country, and result in the publication of allegations made by personal enemies." Having said this, Senator Taft proceeded to consider the constitutional question of the

[15] Ibid., p. 2270.
[16] Ibid., p. 2270.
[17] Ibid., p. 2283.

Senate's right to an independent appraisal of FBI files in the course of confirmation proceedings:

> As I see it, we must take somebody's appraisal of the file. If the executive department chooses Mr. Dulles as the person to give us the appraisal, I see no reason why we should not accept the appraisal by Mr. Dulles. . . .
>
> I do regard with great favor the suggestion that a Senator or Senators should be appointed by the Committee on Foreign Relations to examine the file and give the Senate their appraisal. . . . As I have said, that is not at all because I distrust Mr. Dulles, but because I think the Senate has a constitutional duty of its own, namely, to confirm appointments, which is entirely independent of the appointing power. Therefore, it seems appropriate to me that we should obtain the appraisal of somebody approaching the question from the point of view of the Senate and its power of confirmation. . . .[18]

At last, after prolonged discussion, one member of the Foreign Relations Committee, Senator Guy Gillette of Iowa, gave the Senate the following account of one of the several items of derogatory information about which Secretary Dulles had told the committee in detail:

> One of the derogatory reports—and it was a derogatory report, and Senators may evaluate it, along with members of the Committee on Foreign Relations—concerned a person who said he possessed a sixth sense in addition to the five senses all of us possess. He said that due to his possessing this sixth sense he could look at a man and determine whether or not there was something immoral about him, or something pertaining to moral turpitude in the man's makeup, or some tendency on his part to take action that would not be accepted in good society as moral action. This man said that he looked at Mr. Bohlen and, with this sixth sense of his, he determined that Mr. Bohlen was a man who did have in the back of his mind such a tendency toward immorality as to make him unfit.[19]

Such being the stuff of FBI files, it is small wonder that neither the subject of investigation nor the FBI itself relishes the idea of publication. "There is no one in this room who has ever

[18] Ibid., p. 2283.
[19] Ibid., p. 2285.

amounted to anything, who, if he were investigated, would not have some derogatory remark made about him by some jealous person, some person whom he may have unintentionally injured, someone who is not particularly careful," Senator Wiley told the Senate.[20]

"If the only derogatory material contained in the file on the nominee is that someone is said to have believed that the nominee looked like a potential criminal," said Senator George W. Malone plaintively, "certainly that is not information that a Senator of the United States could not properly obtain and inspect in order to clear up the situation regarding Mr. Bohlen. There must be more to it than that in order for the Secretary of State to refuse access to the members of the Senate." [21]

But apparently there was not more to it than that. In the end Senator Taft's suggestion was adopted and a subcommittee consisting of himself and Senator John Sparkman went over to Secretary Dulles's office to look at the FBI summary, which J. Edgar Hoover assured them was detailed and complete. Dulles stipulated that "the contents will not be disclosed" and that "the executive branch of the government did not consider that this constitutes a precedent so far as it is concerned." The two Senators reported that there was nothing in the summary which had not already been made known to the Foreign Relations Committee by Dulles. With this assurance, the Senate voted to confirm Bohlen by 74 to 13; the affirmative votes came from 39 Democrats, 34 Republicans, and 1 Independent, Senator Wayne Morse of Oregon.

The debate over the confirmation of Ambassador Bohlen highlights the issues in the recurrent conflict between congressional committees and Presidents over access to executive papers. Undoubtedly there are executive files and reports that must be kept confidential—among them, obviously, the files and reports of the FBI. But an over-rigid refusal to give Congress any access to such executive papers may needlessly impede the work of legis-

[20] Ibid., p. 2281.
[21] Ibid., p. 2281.

lation; and it may also upset the constitutional balance of powers by making it impossible for the legislature to impose a check upon the Executive.

The absence of a legislative check—or of any publicity—may promote gross irresponsibility or carelessness in an executive agency—which is especially dangerous in a police agency such as the FBI. So long as its reports are kept confidential, appraisal of its methods, its sources, its reliability, and its judgment is extremely difficult. Moreover, if the Senate is to make of its confirmatory power something more than a ritual—if Congress as a whole is to discharge effectively its role as a censor of the executive branch—then executive papers ought to be withheld only to the extent genuinely necessary to protect the public interest. Surely some of the leaders of Congress can be trusted with the reports that are sent to high officials of the executive branch. Congress itself ought to impose on these leaders an appropriate sense of responsibility and discretion. The President ought to facilitate congressional access to such material, within prudent limits, in a spirit of executive-legislative cooperation.

Discretion and the right of decision regarding executive papers must lie with the President as the head of the executive branch of the government. But these must be guided by a recognition that the executive and legislative branches belong to the same government and are supposed to function as partners. The appropriate rule is the rule that George Washington laid down when the government was in its infancy: "The Executive ought to communicate such papers as the public good would permit and ought to refuse those the disclosure of which would injure the public."

CHAPTER III

CONGRESS AND THE EXECUTIVE

A general, roving, offensive, inquisitorial, compulsory investigation, conducted by a commission without any allegations, upon no fixed principles and governed by no rules of law, or of evidence, and no restraints except its own will, or caprice, is unknown to our Constitution and laws; and such an inquisition would be destructive of the rights of the citizen, and an intolerable tyranny. Let the power once be established, and there is no knowing where the practice under it would end.[1]

I

ON MARCH 28, 1953, Senator Joseph R. McCarthy announced that the Senate Permanent Subcommittee on Investigations of the Committee on Government Operations, of which he was chairman, had negotiated an agreement with the Greek owners of 242 merchant ships to stop trade with North Korea, Communist China, and Russia's Far Eastern ports. The announcement produced headlines of which the Senator was indubitably the hero.

"Negotiation" was the word used by Senator McCarthy in describing his activities; and "agreement" was the term he applied to the outcome. The Senator said that the "agreement" had been worked out by representatives of his subcommittee and he

---

[1] J. Sawyer, *In Re Pacific Ry Commission*, 32 Fed. 241, 263 (1887).

emphasized that it had been concluded with no collaboration whatever from agencies of the executive branch of the government, including the State Department. "I didn't want any interference by anyone," he explained. At the same time he accused the State Department of "dismal failure" in its efforts to reduce shipping to Communist Chinese ports.[2]

On March 29, the day after Senator McCarthy's announcement, officials of the State Department disclosed that the Greek government had agreed within the past ten days to forbid ships operating under the Greek flag to carry cargoes to or from Communist countries. On March 30, a day later, the director of the Mutual Security Agency, Harold E. Stassen, declared that Senator McCarthy's action had the effect of "undermining" this nation's foreign policy, and that it was "harmful to our objective" of negotiating international agreements to eliminate trade with Communist countries. Stassen added that Senator McCarthy's action violated "the whole process of government."

For a short time a rather sharp and interesting clash seemed to be developing between McCarthy and Stassen. The Senator said that the Mutual Security director "advised us the other day to deal directly with the shipowners." Stassen flatly denied this in the course of an appearance before the McCarthy Subcommittee. "No, Senator," he said, "I did not tell that to you. I said if you want to be cooperative and helpful, you should bring out the facts about these owners."

Apparently the Senator was well aware that negotiations through normal diplomatic channels were then in progress between the United States government and the Greek government. The Mutual Security director said that he had told the Senator at an informal conference ten days earlier that "we are moving in on this situation with the Greek owners." He said the McCarthy Subcommittee then proceeded to negotiate with the owners on its own account without advising MSA of what it was doing. And he inquired bluntly whether the Senator obtained

[2] Quotations in connection with Greek shipping incident are from the *Washington Post*.

the agreement by promising the Greek shipowners that he would spare them the discomfort of a public hearing before his subcommittee. From another member of the subcommittee, Senator Karl E. Mundt of South Dakota, there was a candid intimation that this was indeed the case. Senator Mundt told a newspaper reporter it was his guess that the shipowners decided it would be better to sign an agreement to halt trade with Communist areas than "to be hauled down here and have the whole thing ventilated" at public hearings.

The day after the interchange between the Senator and the Mutual Security director the Greek shipowners entered the discussion with a somewhat disconcerting statement. Five of them said they were sure none of their vessels had transported any cargo into Red China or North Korea for at least two years. Their chief reason for signing the agreement, they said, was to eliminate bad publicity after they had been "falsely accused" of delivering goods to the Chinese Communists. It was in any case a somewhat rhetorical agreement. It had no legal effect, and Senator McCarthy's subcommittee had no means of enforcing it.

Up to this point the Secretary of State, normally the negotiator of American foreign relations, had had nothing to say on the subject of the Greek shipowners and their trade with Senator McCarthy. On April 1, however, Secretary Dulles had a luncheon meeting with the Senator, at the conclusion of which a joint statement was issued, more or less in the nature of a communiqué. It was, by any standard, a remarkable statement, and no date could have been more appropriate for its publication than April Fools' Day. It read in part:

It was pointed out the dangers that would result if congressional committees entered into the field of foreign relations, which is in the exclusive jurisdiction of the Chief Executive. Senator McCarthy stated that he was aware of these considerations and had no desire or intention to act contrary to them. . . . Senator McCarthy further pointed out that neither he nor his committee had made or contemplated making any agreements with any foreign governments or foreign shipping groups, but that as a by-product of the committee's investigation, certain foreign shipping groups had voluntarily agreed among themselves to abstain from participation in the Communist Chinese trade and inter-Soviet bloc trade, a result which both Secretary Dulles and Senator McCarthy felt was in the national interest.

Perhaps the most remarkable aspect of this remarkable statement was the dramatic transformation it wrought upon Senator McCarthy. Just prior to his meeting with the Secretary of State he told news reporters that he contemplated the conclusion of a similar agreement with another group of Greek shipowners in London and planned to ask Dulles if he should proceed with these negotiations. "One of the primary things I want to find out," he told reporters as he entered the meeting, "is if he approves of our going ahead with negotiations with the Greek committee in London."

McCarthy talked rather differently, however, when he was interviewed immediately after the meeting. Reporters asked him if he intended to proceed with the London negotiations. The account of the interview by Murrey Marder in the *Washington Post* achieves a level of high comedy:

"I wouldn't say that 'negotiation' is the right word," said McCarthy. "If any group of shipowners agrees to remove their ships from the China trade, we will keep the Secretary informed."

He was pressed to comment on the "negotiations." He replied: "I wouldn't have anything further to say at this particular time."

Reporters asked if he promised Dulles to "call off" the negotiations. "We haven't called anything on or off," replied McCarthy. Are negotiations, then, he was asked, still in progress?

"I don't know what you call 'negotiate,'" replied McCarthy. He was reminded that he had said his subcommittee was "negotiating" with the Greek shipowners in London.

"I don't recall what I said the other day," said McCarthy, asking, "Can I go now?"

A reporter recalled that in his original announcement of the Greek action last Saturday, McCarthy repeatedly described his subcommittee's relations with the shipowners as "negotiations."

"Did we?" asked McCarthy. He rubbed his chin and hesitated.

"Let's put it this way," he finally said. "If and when the London group or any other group voluntarily agrees to remove their ships from the trade, that will be immediately conveyed to the State Department." He said his subcommittee will continue its investigation of shipping in the same manner as before.

At that point one reporter rushed up late. "What about those London negotiations?" he asked. Everyone, including McCarthy, laughed.

Whatever benefits, if any, may have accrued to the country from McCarthy's conversations, arrangements, understandings, or transactions with the Greek shipowners, the significant and striking fact is that he and his subcommittee undertook an executive function. This much he seems to have recognized and acknowledged himself. If business of this sort is to be pursued by the staffs of congressional committees, then there is really little need for large bureaucratic establishments such as the Department of State or the Mutual Security Agency—a realization that may have been responsible for provoking Stassen's indignation.

There are two considerations which argue compellingly against congressional discharge of so characteristically executive a function as the negotiation of an international agreement. One is that the legislative body lacks the skills, the trained and specialized personnel, the detachment from immediate political pressures, the detailed knowledge of particular situations requisite to this sort of undertaking. Even under parliamentary systems, where legislative and executive activities are more merged, a sharp line is drawn between the formulation of policy and the execution of it; the latter is left exclusively to professional civil servants in the several ministries.

If policy were to be executed by those who authorized it, there would be no check upon performance, no counterbalancing of power. And this illuminates the second consideration: that the concentration of executive and legislative powers in a single set of hands would lead inescapably to uncontrolled—which is to say, tyrannical—authority. It was against this threat that the authors of the Constitution sought to safeguard the American people by divorcing legislative from executive operations.

It may fairly be said that no great harm came from McCarthy's little excursion into diplomacy. This is because the executive authorities discerned its potentialities for mischief and diverted it before it could do much damage. It seems clear that Secretary Dulles talked toughly enough to McCarthy in their luncheon interview to send the Senator forth chastened, for once. But the administration avoided an open showdown over the affair and allowed McCarthy to save what face he could. President Eisenhower said at a press conference a day or two after the Dulles-McCarthy meeting that Stassen had overstated the case in charging McCarthy with "undermining" the nation's foreign policy. The President accepted the Senator's assertion that he had not been "negotiating"; he could not have been negotiating, Eisenhower put it blandly, because he had nothing to commit. The Senator, at any rate, negotiated no more.

II

But the insistence on its prerogatives which characterized the executive branch of the government on this occasion and rendered the Senator's invasion innocuous was not evident in connection with another McCarthy foray—his investigation of the International Information Administration. Under the guise of investigation, the Senator's subcommittee virtually took over the management and operation of this agency, which was the State Department's instrument for making the United States and its policy understood and respected overseas. The invasion of executive authority in this instance, if less flagrant than in the case of the Greek shipowners, was more serious; unlike that musical-comedy incident, it met with disastrous success. Before McCarthy got through with it, the overseas information program was pretty completely destroyed.

The McCarthy assault began almost as soon as the Eisenhower administration took office, and mildly enough, with a statement in February 1953 by Senator Mundt that the subcommittee would make an investigation of "bad judgment or worse" in the United States overseas propaganda program. A day later McCarthy, in New York, made it clear that the investigation would center on the "worse" rather than on the "bad judgment." Some people in the New York branch of the Voice of America are doing, he said, "a fairly good job of sabotaging Dulles's and Eisenhower's foreign-policy program."

That the President and the Secretary of State might be better equipped than he to deal with the alleged "sabotage" seems never to have occurred to him. McCarthy interrogated several witnesses in a secret session of the subcommittee in New York and told the press that the day's evidence dealt with "a vast amount of waste, running into tens of millions." The hearings, he declared, would look into possible mismanagement, subversion, waste, and kickbacks in the Voice of America program.

The theme of waste complicated by subversion was reiterated a few days later by another member of the subcommittee, Senator John L. McClellan of Arkansas, who told the press that "more than incompetency or plain stupidity" seemed to be involved in reports of "millions of dollars of waste in constructing broadcasting facilities for the Voice." Considerable publicity was given to the testimony of an assistant chief of the Voice's Domestic Transmitter Section, Donald R. Creed, who told the subcommittee about a mobile radio unit which cost $65,000 to build and then limped along the highways until it had a $30,000 "adjustment." Its steering wheel came loose, all the bolts fell out, it was dangerous to operate, and it was used only twice, according to the witness.

This bit of testimony given in mid-February is significant chiefly because when the printed hearings of the investigation were issued four months later, in June, Creed's charges appeared in a much modified form. Not only was the witness's testimony changed to correct factual inaccuracies, but questions he was asked by subcommittee members were also changed or eliminated in order to bring them into conformity with his amended responses. The printed record made no acknowledgment that the testimony had been substantially altered. Nor did the subcommittee offer any indication that the widely publicized charge of waste in the mobile transmitter unit was quite inaccurate.

It seemed that Creed had somewhat overstated the case against the Voice. The cost of the mobile unit, as he subsequently told the subcommittee, "ran approximately around $41,239.22"—instead of the $65,000 he originally estimated. And the cost of modifying the unit to correct its defects was not $30,000, but $590.

This kind of revision of the record—suggestive of nothing so much as the techniques of rewriting history employed by "Big Brother" in George Orwell's 1984—makes it peculiarly difficult for truth to expose falsehood. Save for an extended but inconclusive discussion as to whether two projected radio transmitters had been prudently located with a view to their broadcasting efficiency, little more was heard about waste and extravagance in the Voice program after Creed's testimony. The hearings thereafter maintained an almost unwavering focus on "subversion."

The method of "investigation" employed by McCarthy was to summon before the committee disgruntled State Department employees and publicize their aspersions on their associates and superiors. There were, of course, the inevitable ex-Communists—for example, Alexander Barmine, a former Soviet Intelligence officer, who fled into exile in 1937 and eventually became head of the Voice of America's Russian desk. He told the subcommittee that Communist leaders had "a pathological fear of Stalin's death," that he himself had prepared a script for the Voice, titled "Stalin's Testament," which capitalized on this fear, but it had been rejected by his superiors. The effectiveness of the Voice in general, he declared, was impaired by "weasel-worded" directives from Washington.

There were other zealous employees of the State Department —non-Communists—who felt that the particular areas of activity with which they were connected were being given inadequate attention in the overseas information program. Sidney Glazer, chief of the Voice of America's Hebrew service, complained to the subcommittee about a decision to suspend Hebrew-language broadcasts to Israel, and Gerald Dooher, chief of the Voice's Near East and Asia service, testified: "To me it was one of the most shocking things I had heard about in my eight years with the organization. It was a well-struck blow for the Communist powers."

Reed Harris, the man responsible for the decision to suspend these particular broadcasts, said that the Voice program reached Israel in languages more widely understood than Hebrew, and that the Voice's limited budget could be utilized more effectively by other forms of anti-Communist propaganda beamed in other directions. The disappointment felt by Glazer and Dooher over the suspension of a program to which they had devoted much thought and effort is readily understandable. Government employees tend to believe that the particular activities in which they are engaged are indispensable to the nation's survival. But perhaps there is room in such a situation for honest differences of opinion—or, at any rate, differences not motivated by any desire to strike a blow for communism. The British also discontinued their broadcasts in Hebrew, without anyone's being accused of being un-British.

The hearing accorded Harris by the McCarthy Subcommittee and the hearing given a few weeks later to Theodore Kaghan, acting deputy director of the Office of Public Affairs of the United States High Commissioner in Germany, afford interesting illustrations of McCarthy's investigating methods. It is difficult to believe that these hearings were held solely for the purpose of obtaining information. They seemed a deliberate effort on the part of the subcommittee to take over the direction of the information program.

McCarthy's technique in dealing with Harris and Kaghan was to exhume from their youthful pasts writings that could be made to seem excruciatingly embarrassing when read aloud at a public hearing and broadcast to thousands of listeners by radio and TV. In the case of Harris, the instrument of torture was a book titled *King Football*, which he had written hurriedly, and ill advisedly, twenty-one years earlier, at the time of his apparently involuntary resignation from Columbia University. It was, judging by the excerpts chosen for audition at the hearing, a book containing, as Harris himself seemed more than ready to acknowledge, a great deal of adolescent foolishness. McCarthy read aloud passages that stated or suggested that the Russian experiment was idyllic, that capitalism was obsolescent, marriage outmoded, and American universities in the grip of a totalitarian tyranny. The Senator quoted such passages redundantly and kept asking Harris blandly whether he still held the same opinions.

In Kaghan's case the torture was even more cruel, since it was applied by reading aloud passages from a play written long ago while he was a student at the University of Michigan. A good deal of the play seems to have been taken up with dialogue between a Communist and a non-Communist. The Communist's speeches, very rhetorical and undoubtedly very anti-capitalist, were persistently recited by the Senator and followed by the query, "Would you say that is the Communist line or not?" Kaghan, troubled by an understandable inability to recollect all the dialogue after the passage of a couple of decades and having no script in front of him at the hearing, could only assert and reassert helplessly, "That would appear to be a Communist speaking." This served only to lead to a stretching of the rack by McCarthy. "I hand you your own play," said the chairman of the subcommittee, "and ask you to read the concluding paragraphs and tell us whether they do not end up with the Communist victorious. Is that not the end of all your plays?"

This sort of public exhibition of one's youthful extravagances is a cruel and unusual punishment. What one writes when young —like what one writes when in love—can be unbearably painful if published years later. Perhaps, indeed, this is why men pay blackmail to recover old love letters; it is not so much that the letters themselves are compromising or that the liaison they reveal is discreditable, as that one cannot bear to have one's forgotten feelings and one's sentimental excesses bared to the world.

In addition to questioning Harris and Kaghan about youthful expressions of opinion, McCarthy also asked them questions about their associations in the distant past. Harris, it appeared, had known a Columbia teacher named Donald Henderson, who subsequently became one of the principal figures in a union ejected from the Congress of Industrial Organizations as Communist-controlled. "Did you know Donald Henderson was a Communist?" McCarthy asked half a dozen times in half a dozen different ways.

Harris responded, "I knew he was a Marxist and not an announced Socialist party member. I therefore would have referred to him as a communist with a lower-case 'c.' But I had no knowledge that he had anything to do with the Communist party. There is a difference there, sir."

The bar sinister of association in Kaghan's case was a man named Ben Irwin, with whom he had shared a room for a time in New York City in the mid-thirties. "You knew Ben Irwin was a Communist at that time, did you not?" the chairman asked. "I assumed he was," said Kaghan.

THE CHAIRMAN: And did Ben Irwin have meetings in your room at the time that you knew he was a member of the Communist party?

MR. KAGHAN: He did not have what were obviously meetings. He had people in. I never recognized them as meetings of an organization. They were people that came to see him, and there were groups there from time to time.

THE CHAIRMAN: You knew he was a Communist. Were the men who attended these, call them what you may, meetings or gatherings, known to you also as members of the Communist party?

MR. KAGHAN: Sir, I did not say I knew he was a Communist. I assumed he was a Communist.

THE CHAIRMAN: All right. When you assumed he was a Communist, did you know anybody else who attended those gatherings in your home that you also assumed were Communists?

MR. KAGHAN: The place was not my home alone. It was also his. And I assumed that some of them probably were Communists. I wasn't afraid of Communists in those days. I didn't know the distinction between communism and political conspiracy.

It was brought out in the hearing that Kaghan had signed a nominating petition for a Communist candidate for councilman of New York City. "I intended to support his attempt to get on the ballot," Kaghan testified. "I did not vote for him. And, as far as I can recall, I didn't do anything to help his election." At that time, the witness explained, he considered communism in America a political party, entitled to election or rejection in the polling booth, and did not recognize it as an international conspiracy. When asked by McCarthy to recall who sought his signature on the nominating petition, Kaghan was unable to do so. Nor could he remember the identity of anybody who urged him to join the Communist party.

The subcommittee's criterion of conversion from collegiate unorthodoxy was a willingness to name others who long ago had shared one's wrongheadedness. The inability or unwillingness of Harris and Kaghan to name associates who twenty years earlier had, like themselves, mistakenly thought of communism as a political party instead of an international conspiracy went strongly against them. The chairman of the committee said to Kaghan:

Mr. Kaghan, when we asked you a question the other day—I have discussed this with a number of Senators since then—we asked you to name some of the other men whom you associated with during those years, at the time you were living with this man you say you assumed was a Communist, when you were writing for this Communist organization; the names of some of the other men that you at that time or now think were members of the Communist party. Your memory was extremely bad. You could not think of a single individual except Irwin who had been exposed as a Communist. May I say that you certainly will not convince me, and I do not think you will convince any other individual here, that you have actually broken with the Communist party unless you come forth now very freely and give us the names of the other individuals with whom you were associated. You have testified, for example, that there were meetings held at the home in which you lived, lived with a man you knew to be a Communist. Your memory is bad. You cannot think of a single one of their names. I am sure there is not a single person in this room but what would remember some of the people he was associated with in 1939 or 1938; and, especially in view of the fact that you were selected by Mr. Acheson or someone in the old State Department to lead the fight against communism in Europe, it seems your memory should be good enough so that you could think of one name of someone who has not been exposed already as a Communist. Is your memory still as bad as it was the other day?

Kaghan seems to have been handicapped not only by a natural reluctance to spew names before the committee, but also by the fact that he had evidently never joined the Communist party and therefore had no former cell mates to identify. "Sir," he said, "the implication that I had any Communist party to break with is one I reject. I was never a member of the Communist party, as I testified. I have shown here I was not even as close to communism as you had me thinking for a while. I didn't have to move to break away from anything. I just moved away from the associations."

But McCarthy was insistent. "Can you," he demanded, "give us the name of one individual that you thought then or think now was a Communist? You said you attended, I believe, roughly a dozen meetings, Communist meetings. I would like to know who was there, and whether you went to the FBI and gave the FBI the names of the members who attended those meetings. I know many of them attended under false names, but even then it would help. You have not done that, have you?"

Recounting his experience in a magazine article some months later, Kaghan observed that "the fact that I hadn't belonged to any Communist cell and therefore hadn't known who was really a Communist and who wasn't in those days seemed to make no difference. To assure a friendly response in public from a Senator, I had to buy him with names, and I didn't have any names to offer beyond the one Communist I was sure of." [3] It is impossible to escape a feeling that some of McCarthy's witnesses did not share Kaghan's scruples.

Harris and Kaghan defended themselves before the subcommittee as ably as men could in a period when scruples of this kind had only a nostalgic, sentimental value. The State Department was not much interested in scruples. It was interested in placating powerful senators. This meant that Harris, the number two man in the overseas information program, and generally considered its ablest executive, and Kaghan, who had won wide respect for his anti-Communist work in Austria and Germany, had to be

[3] "The McCarthyization of Theodore Kaghan," *The Reporter*, July 21, 1953.

sacrificed. They were allowed to resign, but under circumstances that made the Department's humiliation painfully apparent.

It seems fair to say that the vanquished in these encounters were not Kaghan and Harris so much as the Department of State itself. The significant point was not the ruin of a couple of promising governmental careers but the Department's surrender to a species of legislative extortion. Responsibility for the conduct of the foreign information program belongs in the executive branch of the government. But the executive branch sloughed off this responsibility—or at least allowed McCarthy to assume it. In doing so it broke down the wall which the Constitution established between executive and legislative functions.

Having reduced the Voice of America to a gurgle, the McCarthy Subcommittee shifted its attention from the spoken to the printed word. The inquiry into the management and operations of the overseas information program reached a disastrous culmination in the purging or burning of books in the overseas libraries and ended by reducing these libraries to mere propaganda outlets. It cannot fairly be said that the Senator was directly responsible for these excesses. As he observed himself, with an obvious sense of injured innocence, "I haven't burned any books since, as a kid on the farm, I used to start fires for my Ma each morning with old newspapers, magazines, and so on." It is a tribute, nevertheless, to McCarthy's power that fear of him led the State Department into issuing a succession of extremely confusing and intimidating directives to the librarians in charge of overseas libraries; and these led the librarians to commit acts of timorous folly, if not of downright vandalism.

Early in the probe of the International Information Administration the counsel of the subcommittee, Roy Cohn, produced a State Department memorandum dated February 3, 1953, entitled "Information Policy for Use of Material by Controversial Persons." It said in part: "The reputation abroad of an author affects the actual utility of the material. If he is widely and favorably known as a champion of democratic causes, his credibility and utility may be enhanced. Similarly, if—like Howard Fast—he is known as a Soviet-indorsed author, materials favorable to the United States may be given a special credibility among selected key audiences."

This would seem to be a sensible enough policy, on the premise that anti-Communist propaganda might carry special weight when attributable to someone known to be pro-Communist. Testimonials from critics generally have greater effectiveness than the praise of friends. The day after McCarthy's discovery of the State Department's memorandum, however, the Department issued what came to be known as the "et cetera order," halting the use in any of its overseas information programs of material by any "controversial" author accused of being a Communist or "fellow-traveler." The order read in part: "In order to avoid all misunderstanding, no material by any controversial persons, Communists, fellow-travelers, et cetera, will be used under any circumstances by any International Information Administration media." The State Department, it appeared, had become as susceptible as any advertising sponsor to intimidation by blacklisting.

This was the first in a series of abject State Department surrenders to McCarthy's pressures. A day later the Department rescinded an earlier order which authorized any employee to decide for himself whether he would talk "informally" with committee investigators without a senator's being present. McCarthy asserted that this would "hamstring" his investigation of the Voice of America, and the Department allowed him to have his way. It is hard to see in this anything but an outright abdication of executive responsibility. For a considerable period from this time forward, Senator McCarthy became, in effect, the director of the IIA program. He was given, in short, a free hand in what turned out to be a wrecking operation.

Early in March 1953 the IIA acquired a new director, Dr. Robert L. Johnson, a conservative Republican who had become a millionaire as one of the initial organizers of Time, Inc., and who had moved on to the presidency of Temple University. His principal aide was a successful businessman, Martin Merson, who subsequently recounted the disillusioning experience of their five months as government administrators. "Both of us," said Mr. Merson, "wanted close and friendly relations with McCarthy."[4] But close and friendly relations with McCarthy, they found, involved doing his bidding with absolute docility in the firing—and hiring —of employees and in removing from the shelves of overseas libraries thirty thousand copies of books which the Senator said were by "Communist authors." Most of the books he wanted purged were by such authors as Elmer Davis, John Dewey, Zechariah Chafee, Jr., Sherwood Anderson, Stephen Vincent Benét, Edna Ferber, Archibald MacLeish, and a host of other respected and distinguished writers.

The bewildered administrators found no help in the administration. According to Merson, they appealed to Dulles, in whose Department the IIA was an agency, "but the Secretary seemed to want to wash his hands of the whole business." They sought an interview with the President, but were told that he was solidly booked for two weeks. They turned for help to C. D. Jackson, the President's closest adviser on psychological warfare. They asked him, says Merson, "to go to the President to request his support if we told McCarthy and his henchmen that enough was enough. But Jackson blandly answered that he wouldn't dream of approaching the President on the subject. It was Eisenhower's 'passion,' he reminded me, 'not to offend anybody in Congress.' "[5]

Testifying in June before the House Government Operations Committee—not to be confused with McCarthy's Senate Committee on Government Operations—Johnson acknowledged that confusion over State Department directives regarding books and materials in the overseas libraries "has brought great discredit to this administration and to this country." He resigned his office on July 6 because of ill health, after completing a new set of instructions governing the use of material in the overseas libraries. The new policy abandoned the general prohibition against books by Communist or fellow-traveler authors and instituted a test of

[4] "A Businessman's Education in Government," *The Reporter,* October 7, 1954.
[5] Ibid.

suitability on the basis of content. The new test, Dr. Johnson declared somewhat vaguely, will be whether the books serve "the ends of democracy. We in America have nothing to hide. We want the world to know us just as we are. . . . Let totalitarian nations advertise the fact that their people are deprived of political dissent." American prestige might have been spared an uncomfortable blow had this test been applied before advertising the restraints on political dissent adopted at the behest of Senator McCarthy.

"Basically," Johnson said, "the yardstick for selection is the usefulness of a particular book in meeting the particular needs of a particular area. We must begin with the content of a book. . . . It is conceivable that the special purpose character of our libraries may require, in special cases, the inclusion of books by Communists or Communist sympathizers, if such authors may have written affirmatively something which serves the ends of democracy." He added that we "cannot disregard the reputation or standing of the author," and made it plain that leftist political affiliations would not be conducive to inclusion on the overseas library shelves. But he said specifically that some books by mystery writers or humorists who happened to be Communists or pro-Communists would be granted space provided they had "nothing to do with communism."

McCarthy was not slow to recognize that the new criterion put the library program back on its original basis. The day after the revised policy was announced the Senator summoned Johnson and other IIA officials to appear before his Senate subcommittee to defend what he called their "completely ridiculous" new policy. He ordered the retiring administrator specifically to "have present the individual or individuals responsible for the decision to continue the purchase of books by Communist authors."

Johnson, in the manner of a man who no longer had anything to gain by placating the Senator from Wisconsin, came back with a broadside. "One of the great dangers I have sensed during my term of office," he said, "is that many of our most effective programs are being impaired by unsupported charges that they are somehow soft on communism. I do not say that there is a deliberate effort to kill or cripple these anti-Communist programs through the simple device of making such charges. I merely point out that it is one of the tragic ironies of our time that some of those who are in the forefront of the fight against communism are among those who are damaging the action programs that do battle against it."

Apparently pleased with the results of his newly acquired temerity, Johnson let loose once more a couple of days later in response to a charge made by Karl Baarslag, newly appointed research director for the McCarthy Subcommittee. Baarslag was quoted in a newspaper interview as saying that the overseas libraries "just don't go in for anti-Soviet literature," and that on a recent European inspection he was unable to locate "anything in the nature of anti-Soviet publications." Johnson said flatly that Baarslag's statement was "patently false and clearly damaging to the vital interest of the American people abroad," and he added for good measure that it was "flagrantly inaccurate" and "completely dishonest or downright malicious."

McCarthy's reaction was quick and characteristic. The Senator, in addition to being chairman of the Committee on Government Operations, was chairman of the Senate Appropriations Subcommittee on the State Department, with jurisdiction over funds for the IIA. "Doctor," he said to Johnson, "if you had deliberately set out to sabotage any possibility of getting adequate funds to run a good information program, you could not have done a better job in that sabotage than you have. . . . You have done almost irreparable damage to the possibility of obtaining adequate funds for an information program which could be a real Voice of America and not a voice for Moscow, as it has been to such a great extent under the previous administration." What McCarthy proposed to do, apparently, was to cut out the Voice of America's tongue to spite Dr. Johnson's face.

III

With this triumph over the State Department behind him, Senator McCarthy looked for new conquests. The Department of the Army showed no greater disposition or capacity to hold him in.

The Senator undertook an investigation of Army Intelligence in connection with a secret report on Soviet Siberia that warned Intelligence officers against assuming that the whole population of the Soviet Union was ready to rise in revolt against its Communist masters. The document, entitled "Psychological and Cultural Traits of Soviet Siberia," was prepared by the Army's Far East Command on the basis of interviews with repatriated Japanese war prisoners. McCarthy charged that some of the authors whose writings were included in the bibliography of the report were Communists and received instructions from Moscow. He produced three witnesses against the report. Igor Bogolepov, who identified himself as a former member of the Soviet Foreign Office, said he considered the report "extremely dangerous." Vladimir Petrov, a former Soviet subject who said he served six years in a Siberian prison before World War II, denounced the author of the report as "certainly at least a fool, and at worst a traitor." And Louis Budenz, whose attendance at obsequies of this sort had become almost *de rigueur,* expressed an opinion that the report was "the work of a concealed Communist."

McCarthy's chief target, as it turned out, was not the unidentified major who had written the report but Major General Richard C. Partridge, chief of Army Intelligence, who had had the temerity to defend the report in a closed hearing of the McCarthy Investigating Subcommittee. At a subsequent open hearing McCarthy asked Budenz, "Would you say that if the head of Army Intelligence said, 'I believe all of this material,' would you say that would give an extremely dangerous position?" So primed, Budenz obligingly responded, "I hesitate to pass on a gentleman in that position, but since you put the question, I would say it would be very dangerous to the security of the United States."

This was the end of the matter—except that three weeks later the Army announced that General Partridge had been replaced as chief of Military Intelligence and shifted to Europe for assignment by Army authorities there.

Appetite, the French say, comes with eating. McCarthy next undertook an investigation into alleged espionage at the Army Signal Corps' radar base at Fort Monmouth, New Jersey. At the outset McCarthy told reporters, according to an Associated Press story datelined October 12, 1953, that secret testimony given before his subcommittee "has all the earmarks that extremely dangerous espionage" has been committed recently at Fort Monmouth and that "if it develops as it has been, it will envelop the whole Signal Corps."

The Associated Press quoted him on October 15 as recounting the testimony of a German radar scientist that "the Russians said they could get anything they wanted out of Fort Monmouth." On October 19, McCarthy told reporters about an unidentified German scientist who, after escaping from the Russian Zone of Germany, said he had seen "many microfilmed copies of documents" from Fort Monmouth. On November 5 he announced that a witness before a secret session of his subcommittee—a woman —had without question "engaged in espionage in the Signal Corps at Fort Monmouth," and asserted that the Rosenberg spy ring (broken by the FBI in 1950) might still be active at Fort Monmouth.

The manner in which these titillating spy stories were brought to public notice illuminates McCarthy's methods. The three Democratic members of the subcommittee [6] had resigned some months earlier in protest against the high-handed way in which the chairman operated. The inquiry at Fort Monmouth was conducted

[6] These were Senators John L. McClellan of Arkansas, W. Stuart Symington of Missouri, and Henry M. Jackson of Washington. The other Republican subcommittee members were Senators Karl E. Mundt of South Dakota, Everett M. Dirksen of Illinois, and Charles E. Potter of Michigan.

by McCarthy singlehanded—as a one-man subcommittee of the subcommittee. The sessions were closed to press and public; but at the conclusion of each day's testimony he obligingly gave newsmen a "summary" of the developments. "At his own discretion," Marquis Childs observed in his column, "the Senator determines what shall or shall not be released from executive sessions, using innuendo and insinuation to make headlines when the material his investigators provide does not measure up to expectations." [7]

Prior to the McCarthy hearings, both the Army and the FBI had conducted exhaustive inquiries into security at Fort Monmouth. At the conclusion of these inquiries Secretary of the Army Robert T. Stevens held a press conference at which he stated flatly, "We have been unable to find anything relating to espionage."

McCarthy responded to this by announcing that he would hold public hearings in order to let "the people hear the testimony regarding espionage at Fort Monmouth." But thereafter, in much the manner of his retreat regarding the "negotiations" with the Greek shipowners, he suddenly began to forget that he had ever talked about espionage. "It isn't our job to develop any espionage case," he told reporters.

The Army was bewilderingly patient and cooperative with McCarthy throughout the course of his Fort Monmouth investigation. Shortly after Secretary Stevens' declaration at a press conference that the Army had been unable to find anything relating to espionage, he had lunch with the Senator in New York and afterward gave another interview in which he blurred the issue and conveyed an impression of friendly cooperation with all that McCarthy was doing. Civilian employees at Fort Monmouth were dismissed or suspended on the flimsiest evidence and the vaguest charges, and the Army did nothing to protect them from the Senator's inquisition.

With the Army apparently content to see itself kicked around and with no one in authority willing to stand up for its honor and integrity, McCarthy grew more and more imperious, more and

[7] *Washington Post*, December 15, 1953.

more reckless, in his accusations and denunciations. The Fort
Monmouth hearings culminated in his disgraceful abuse of Briga-
dier General Ralph W. Zwicker over the honorable discharge that
had been granted to a major who had pleaded the Fifth Amendment. This humiliation of an honored officer at last shocked
Stevens into some realization of his responsibilities.

The Secretary announced that he would no longer allow his
subordinates to be subjected to such treatment. But again the
President's "passion not to offend anybody in Congress" pre-
vailed. Stevens was persuaded by administration leaders to back
down ingloriously. And no doubt appeasement would have continued if McCarthy had not insisted upon abject and total surrender. The conflict had become too bitter to be suppressed; it
ended in the gaudy Army-McCarthy hearings, conducted by Mc-
Carthy's own subcommittee under the temporary chairmanship
of Senator Mundt. For more than a month the committee wrangled
not over the tremendous constitutional issues involved in Mc-
Carthy's attack upon the executive branch of the government, but
over the question whether he had improperly sought special
treatment for an Army private. The whole affair was spectacularly
reduced to its non-essentials.

IV

If congressional investigation is an indispensable check upon
executive authority, its proper exercise is certainly not to frustrate executive discretion and paralyze executive action. Con-
structive cooperation between investigating committees and executive agencies is by no means impossible. In the course of World
War II the Senate War Investigating Committee, commonly
known as the Truman Committee, demonstrated how faithfully
congressional investigators can fulfill a watchdog function without impeding or embarrassing the discharge of executive responsibilities. When the Truman Committee discovered extravagances
or errors in military administration, its chairman did not rush to
a press conference; he called Army administrators to explain the

situation to the committee (presuming them to be honest men and patriots, though not infallible) and gave them a chance to correct improper conditions. The aim of the committee was not to destroy the reputations of executive officials or to inflate the reputations of the committee members, but to promote economy and efficiency.

The Armed Services Preparedness Subcommittee under the chairmanship of Senator Lyndon B. Johnson of Texas carried on this tradition. Its aims were expressed by the chief counsel, Donald C. Cook: "The subcommittee endeavors to avoid second-guessing by refusing to establish itself as a Monday-morning quarterback club of battlefield strategy. It does not tell generals and admirals how to fight, but, rather, makes certain that they and the men fighting under them have what they need to win battles." [8]

At the very time McCarthy was conducting his investigation of the Voice of America, a serious and comparatively sober study of the Voice program was being conducted by a subcommittee of the Senate Foreign Relations Committee under Senator Bourke B. Hickenlooper. The Hickenlooper group found the Voice to be an indispensable instrument of American diplomacy and made a number of recommendations concerning its content and administration. But by the time this report was completed the Voice had little timbre left in it.

The differences between the two investigations are of considerable importance. While the Hickenlooper group exercised an indubitable congressional authority to inquire into the fashion in which an executive agency had discharged its responsibilities, and did so searchingly and critically, the McCarthy group inquired merely into the opinions and political pasts of individual agency employees. Both groups in a sense aimed to affect policy, but one did it by examining performance with a view toward enacting remedial legislation if necessary; the other did it by coercion, which drove out of the agency employees whose ideas the committee disliked. The State Department yielded nothing of its independence to the Hickenlooper investigation; it bowed in servility to McCarthy.

But the fact is that, commonly, investigations of the executive branch concern themselves with personalities. Congress has shown a steady disposition to interfere in precisely the area where the President is most clearly entitled to autonomy under the Constitution—in the selection of personnel through whose activities he must discharge his obligation to "take care that the laws be faithfully executed."

The House of Representatives has always been somewhat jealous about the senatorial prerogative of advice and consent in connection with presidential appointments. And both Houses of Congress have had a pronounced tendency to extend advice and consent to the appointment of inferior officers, whom the President or the heads of Departments are empowered by law to choose at their own discretion. Congress has been disposed, in short, to take the view that positions for which it appropriates salaries should be filled only by officials of whom it approves.

The most egregious attempt to control executive appointments was made by the House in 1943 when it attached a rider to an appropriations bill forbidding the payment of salaries to three named executive employees, Robert Morss Lovett, Goodwin Watson, and William E. Dodd, Jr. These three were among the thirty-nine individuals called "irresponsible, unrepresentative, crackpot radical bureaucrats" by Representative Martin Dies of Texas, then chairman of the House Committee on Un-American Activities; they were given a legislative trial by another House committee and found guilty. But the Supreme Court in 1946 ruled that the measure striking them from the federal payroll was unconstitutional because it amounted to a bill of attainder. The court, however, felt no need to determine whether the case involved, as its critics also charged, a legislative invasion of executive jurisdiction. A compelling argument could be made along this line—and, indeed, was made in some of the briefs presented in behalf of the three men. It would be hard to imagine a more flagrant violation of the constitutional separation of powers than this legislative attempt to dictate the selection of executive personnel. The Chief Executive can scarcely be held responsible for executive conduct unless he is, in fact, responsible for the selection of his subordinates.

Despite this consideration and despite the vigor with which the court rebuked the House for its proscription of Lovett, Dodd, and Watson, congressional committees went right on conducting legislative trials of government employees. It soon became clear that the committees could effectively accomplish their purpose of proscribing individual executive employees without resorting to legislation, which could be struck down by the courts; they could accomplish the same result by mere "investigation." The "exposure" of a man in a public hearing through accusation by some former Communist served to make his continued employment extremely difficult. Denial of the charge was usually of small avail; the suspicion stuck. And the rule was to resolve all such cases of "doubt" in "favor of the government"—as though the interest of the government lay in a callous disregard of the interest of individual citizens.

So successful was the House Committee on Un-American Activities in its techniques of dismissal by "exposure" that in 1950 it won the accolade of imitation. The late Senator Pat McCarran of Nevada, chairman of the powerful Judiciary Committee, established a subcommittee on internal security and naturally established himself as its chairman. The new group took the headlines away from its House counterpart with a systematic and successful effort to purge from the State Department all the career Foreign Service officers who, in the 1940s, had warned that the Chinese Nationalist government of Chiang Kai-shek was a weak reed to rely on and that, as a condition of continued American aid, it should be required to broaden and democratize the base of its representation—the view taken, incidentally, by General George C. Marshall. Loyalty to Chiang was made the test of suitability for service in the Division of Far Eastern Affairs.

Congress has a natural, perhaps an incurable, tendency to interfere in the discharge of executive responsibilities. The tendency can be arrested only through vigilant and resolute insistence by the Chief Executive on all his prerogatives. The issue was apparently recognized by President Eisenhower at the very beginning of his administration. He sought to prevent congressional interference with, and surveillance of, his subordinates by asserting, in his first message to Congress on the State of the Union, that the determination of the fitness of executive employees was an executive responsibility with which Congress ought not to interfere—at least so long as the President enjoyed its confidence. He said:

Confident of your understanding and cooperation, I know that the primary responsibility for keeping out the disloyal and the dangerous rests squarely upon the executive branch. When this branch so conducts itself as to require policing by another branch of the government, it invites its own disorder and confusion.

I am determined to meet this responsibility of the Executive.

Not long after his inauguration the President found it necessary to reject a demand by McCarthy that an official of the Central Intelligence Agency, William P. Bundy, come before his committee to be examined as to whether he was a "security risk." The head of the CIA, Allen Dulles, declined to permit Bundy to go before the committee as a witness. He based this refusal on the ground that the CIA was a highly secret organization whose operations must be kept under cover. This was, as Walter Lippmann astutely pointed out in a newspaper column, a specious and untenable plea. Every agency of the government carries on operations of a confidential or secret character which ought not to be entrusted to employees of doubtful security, and Congress has the right to expect that appropriate security precautions be observed. But the President, having instituted what he deemed appropriate security precautions, had the right to expect Congress to repose some reasonable measure of trust in his discretion. Mr. Lippmann stated it this way:

The true ground for refusing to let Mr. Bundy be examined was not that he works for Allen Dulles rather than John Foster Dulles. It was that no one in this vale of tears can administer any branch of any government decently and successfully if his authority and responsibility in relation to his subordinates are not upheld and maintained.

The right position, then, was to insist that Mr. Bundy is accountable to Mr. Allen Dulles, not to Senator McCarthy or to Congress, and that Mr. Dulles is accountable to the President for the performance of the CIA and, under the President's constitutional authority and prerogative, to the Congress.[9]

The "primary responsibility for keeping out the disloyal and the dangerous rests squarely," as President Eisenhower said, "upon the executive branch." During his first two years in office the assertion proved to be an empty one, for the legislative branch persistently sought and was allowed to police the personnel of the executive branch. It produced thereby a vast amount of "disorder and confusion." What is worse, it permitted a corrosion and corruption of the integrity and independence of the executive branch. It is an essential part of the President's responsibility to resist every invasion of his jurisdiction and every usurpation of his authority. There is no other way to maintain a system of balanced powers.

[9] "Today and Tomorrow," *Washington Post*, July 31, 1953.

CHAPTER IV

CONGRESS AND THE COURTS

There is no liberty, if the judiciary power be not separated from the legislative and executive. Were it joined with the legislative, the life and liberty of the subject would be exposed to arbitrary control; for the judge would be then the legislator. Were it joined to the executive power, the judge might behave with violence and oppression.[1]

I

THE OUTSTANDING theatrical production of the 1950–51 season was, by general acknowledgment, the Kefauver Committee inquiry into interstate crime. The show went on tour, scoring a success in the provinces before it came to New York. In New Orleans, St. Louis, San Francisco, Los Angeles, and Detroit, the hearings conducted by the committee were televised by local stations. The tryouts having proved successful beyond anyone's hopes or expectations, the show was given a national network when it reached New York. Millions of Americans watched the Kefauver Committee's proceedings, following its disclosures from day to day as fascinatedly as though they were successive episodes in a movie serial or a comic strip.

The show had humor as well as melodrama; it was painstak-

[1] Montesquieu, *Spirit of the Laws*, Book XI, Chap. 3, quoted by Edward S. Corwin, *The President* (New York: New York University Press, 1948), pp. 8–9.

ingly staged and directed, so that each day's curtain came down with a promise of fresh sensations in the next installment; its dramatis personae ranged from clowns to sinister witnesses to inquisitors who became household familiars—the committee counsel, Rudolph Halley, solemnly insistent behind his horn-rimmed spectacles; Senator Charles W. Tobey of New Hampshire, sternly moral and homiletic; Senator Estes Kefauver of Tennessee, an oversize owl, benign and bland and forever genial. Halley, previously unknown, became a candidate for the mayoralty of New York, and Senator Kefauver was catapulted from obscurity to consideration for the presidency. It was said at the time that television made Senator Kefauver; but perhaps it would have been equally accurate to say that Senator Kefauver made television.

The Kefauver investigation illustrates the theory that an investigating committee can serve as an adjunct to the informing function of Congress. The principal subject of the committee's concern was gambling. But gambling is essentially a local matter, whatever interstate ramifications it may have. Gambling is not a federal crime; it transgresses state laws or municipal ordinances. Congress can legislate concerning it only in a limited way. "There are lots of things the federal government can do to help," Senator Kefauver observed in an interview, "but, as I said in the beginning, I think ninety-five per cent of it is a local problem, but we can show the way. It's something that is going to require an all-out effort of federal government, state and local governments. But unless the people are interested, none of them will do much good." [2]

Getting the people interested may well be a useful accomplishment of a congressional investigation. The Kefauver Committee certainly did this. It gave the public glimpses of an underworld, morbid yet exciting. It brought notorious newspaper personalities to life and presented them for public inspection. It illuminated

[2] Interview with Senator Estes Kefauver, U.S. *News & World Report*, April 20, 1951.

the relationship between crime and police corruption, the ways in which public apathy brings criminal elements into political power. "Most of our officials and enforcement officers are honest," Senator Kefauver observed. "But the good average citizen should remember that the criminal interests see that their people register and vote. This and bribery are the source of their power." [3]

The Kefauver crime investigation differed from most of the congressional probes into communism in two respects. In the first place, at nearly every stage it showed evidence of careful preparation. Much of the questioning was done, as it should be done, by committee counsel—instead of by various members of the committee vying with one another for publicity and prominence and changing the subject from question to question, as in most of the sessions on subversion. Unlike the heretic-hunters, whose questions were usually random and often merely rhetorical, Halley seemed usually to know what he was looking for. His staff had done such painstaking research into old income-tax returns and real-estate transactions, into earlier state investigations and criminal records, that he led his witnesses skillfully into admission of what he already had learned or surmised. For the most part the committee listened and pondered the testimony.

The second respect in which this investigation differed from those into communism was that it purported to be directed primarily at a legitimate investigative purpose—the discovery of a general condition rather than the exposure, judgment, and punishment of an individual witness. At the same time, however, it must be recognized that the Kefauver investigation trespassed on individual rights in ways which raised questions of the gravest significance.

"We want it distinctly understood," said Senator Kefauver at the opening of a hearing in New York on March 12, 1951, "that we have no prosecutive status. This is not a grand jury. We do not want to cause anybody any trouble if we can help it. We are here to get the facts. We ask the cooperation of the witnesses and of

[3] Ibid.

the public in trying to give this Senate committee such facts that we can present the picture to Congress, and upon which Congress can pass legislation."

But the Kefauver Committee was questioning witnesses, some of whom had criminal records, some of whom were at that very time engaged in violations of the law, some of whom were under investigation for income-tax evasions or other failures to comply with federal or state requirements. To expect candor and cooperation from such witnesses was to expect a great deal. To examine their financial affairs was to expose them to possible prosecution—and, so far as they were concerned individually, to act very much like a grand jury.

It is questionable whether a committee of Congress should act in this way at all or make such demands upon witnesses. Congress does not ordinarily need the testimony of suspected criminals in order to legislate effectively against crime; what Congress needs to know for this purpose can be obtained from the testimony of law-enforcement officers, sociologists, ministers, bar associations, and other reputable sources willing to come forward and testify voluntarily. So far as the committee's role in furthering the informing function of Congress is concerned, it cannot be said to warrant compelling persons to make admissions that are self-debasing if not self-incriminating. The exposure of individual wrongdoing, as Senator Kefauver recognized, is not a function of congressional committees; it is a function of grand juries; and so is the exposure of crime generally.

The truth is that the Kefauver investigation aroused less indignation than the "subversive" probes largely because its witnesses were disreputable persons associated in the public mind with the underworld, instead of respected government employees, teachers, and clergymen; and it was concerned with gambling and racketeering rather than with beliefs and associations. But the infringement of individual rights was hardly less flagrant and hardly less dangerous to American justice. As Justice Frankfurter once observed in a notable dissenting opinion: "Rights intended to protect all must be extended to all, lest they so fall into desuetude in the course of denying them to the worst of men as to afford no aid to the best of men in time of need." [4]

The distinction between a congressional investigating committee and a grand jury, often blurred in practice, is a vitally important one. Like a grand jury, an investigating committee is an instrument of inquiry, but beyond this coincidence there is no similarity. The function of the investigating committee is to inquire into general conditions, while the function of the grand jury is to inquire into specific violations of law.

Because the grand jury is concerned with individual cases and conducts its inquiries as a preliminary to judicial trials, it operates in secret. The Fifth Amendment to the Constitution provides among other things that no person shall be held to answer for an infamous crime except on a presentment or indictment of a grand jury. The purpose of this precaution is, of course, to protect innocent persons from unfounded accusations. If accusations concerning an individual are found by the grand jury to be insubstantial, they are dismissed without any publicity whatever; and indeed it is of the essence of the grand-jury system that the jurors themselves and all those connected with the proceedings are sworn to secrecy.

Legislative hearings, far from providing any comparable protection against unjust charges, give a privileged forum to accusers and serve as a sounding board for their accusations. They give publicity to allegations which a grand jury would keep confidential until they had been weighed and found to have substance. Frequently committee members have tried to gloss over this carelessness by asserting that they afforded individuals called before them a chance to clear themselves before the greatest court in the country—the court of public opinion. They have sought to excuse the absence of procedural safeguards on the ground that the committee does not hand down a formal conviction or impose a formal sentence. Nevertheless, a congressional hearing may destroy an individual's reputation quite as effectively as any court of law; and it may result, in addition, in the loss of his livelihood. It can

[4] *Goldman* v. *United States*, 316 U.S. 129, 142 (1942).

scarcely be a matter of indifference that a committee of Congress should impose such hardships on anyone without affording him an opportunity to call witnesses in his behalf or cross-examine his accusers, without excluding from the hearing incompetent testimony which would be inadmissible in a court of law, and without any attempt at the kind of impartiality that is an essential characteristic of a court.

Abe Fortas, a distinguished Washington lawyer with broad experience in regard to congressional investigations, said of them: "There are no standards of judgment, no rules, no traditions of procedure or judicial demeanor, no statute of limitations, no appeals, no boundaries of relevance, and no finality. In short, anything goes; and everything frequently does—and often on television." [5]

Legislative hearings involving charges against individuals amount, in effect, to trials in which the concept of due process has been abandoned; and, in addition, they sometimes foreclose or impair the granting of due process to persons who are brought to trial subsequently in a court of law. Procedures that are adequate for the legitimate purposes of congressional investigation are entirely inadequate when the investigation involves charges against individuals.

II

The line between investigation and trial is a tenuous one. Congressional inquiry necessarily involves the interrogation of individuals. When someone's testimony is injurious to his reputation, the inquiry takes on for him the nature of a prosecution. The distinction between legislative and judicial functions and the incompetence of committees to discharge the work of courts has been lucidly explained by Professor Zechariah Chafee, Jr., of the Harvard Law School.

[5] Abe Fortas, "Outside the Law," *The Atlantic Monthly*, August 1953, p. 43.

The two outstanding points about legislative investigating committees are that they are well suited to pass on general questions and badly suited for the decision of individual cases. By general questions, I mean the collection of large masses of information which may show the need for new statutes and how new laws ought to be wisely drafted. And I mean more than preparation for legislation. These committees enable Congress to review the past expenditure of vast sums of taxpayers' money and to keep a constant watch upon the conduct of public officials. . . . Congress should be free to choose the ways for carrying out these important tasks. That is what Congress is for.

On the other hand, Congress was not designed to determine whether an individual is innocent or guilty of crime or other misconduct. That is what courts are for. Hence the constitutional prohibition of bills of attainder. And a congressional committee is just as unfit for this task as the whole House. . . . Judges are kept impartial by professional training, the customary safeguards of the courtroom, and the ingrained traditions of the bench. No such factors operate on the men who sit in the Capitol. They are sent there by the people to do a very different job from that of judges, a job that demands very different qualities. Consequently congressmen and senators should, so far as possible, keep away from the judges' job of passing on the guilt of individuals.[6]

This absence of the interplay that characterizes adversary proceedings in a court of law is what makes a congressional hearing totally inadequate for determining the guilt or innocence of an individual. Cross-examination, which Dean John H. Wigmore, the acknowledged authority on evidence, characterized as "beyond doubt the greatest legal engine ever invented for the discovery of truth," is not always feasible in a legislative proceeding. It would slow the pace of investigation and distract the attention of investigators from the general picture upon which a legislative inquiry should be focused. But the lack of it makes altogether impossible the fair determination of what should never be the business of a legislative inquiry—the guilt or innocence of an individual.

Increasingly during the past decade investigating committees

[6] See his Foreword in Alan Barth, *The Loyalty of Free Men* (New York: The Viking Press, 1951), pp. xii, xiii.

have been acting in ways that directly interfere with the functions of courts of law, or have usurped those functions, arrogating to themselves the authority to judge and condemn individuals. The trend has been accelerated and exacerbated by new instruments of publicity. Radio, television, and motion-picture cameras, customarily excluded from law courts, are often admitted to congressional hearings. They raise obvious problems for witnesses. It is not easy or comfortable for everyone to testify before an audience of millions; and the presence of so vast an audience at once puts constraints on witnesses and invites theatrics on the part of the investigators.

Manifestly there are types of congressional investigation in which publicity has great social value and promotes the informing function of Congress. When committees are inquiring into broad public problems and receiving the testimony of experts, it is extremely useful to reach as wide an audience as possible. In such hearings witnesses are unlikely to be under fire themselves or to use the immunity from suits for slander conferred by the committee to make scandalous statements regarding other persons. It is when an accused person is summoned before a committee and compelled to answer charges which have brought him into odium that excessive publicity may infringe his rights. Precisely this kind of hearing is of course the one that is accorded the greatest popular attention.

When Frank Costello came before the Kefauver Committee in New York on March 13, 1951, his attorney, George Wolf, objected "strenuously" to having the proceedings televised. "Upon what basis do you register objection?" asked Senator Herbert R. O'Conor, who was presiding. "On the ground," Mr. Wolf replied, "that Mr. Costello doesn't care to submit himself as a spectacle. And on the further ground that it will prevent proper conference with his attorney, in receiving proper advice from his attorney during the course of the testimony."

Senator O'Conor ruled that Mr. Wolf's objection should be respected, although the ruling contained an interesting Freudian slip: "Well, under the circumstances, then, it is the view of the committee, Counsel, that the defendant not be televised, or the individual who is here, the witness, not be televised at the time." Radio was to be permitted, however, with the proviso that client and counsel should be able to confer "without its being audible to anyone else." [7]

The impact of sensational publicity on the rights of individuals appearing before congressional committees has caused a good deal of concern to thoughtful members of the bar. The Association of the Bar of the City of New York has urged, for instance, that no photographs, moving pictures, television, or radio broadcasts of proceedings be permitted while any witness is testifying. This would impose restraints, to be sure, on elements of the press and on the public's right to information about governmental activities—restraints which certainly ought not to be imposed lightly or frivolously. They seem preferable, however, to the serious trespass on individual rights that may follow from a failure to impose them.

The tradition of public trial grew out of regard for the rights of individuals rather than regard for the public's right to information. The provision of the Bill of Rights that in criminal prosecutions the accused shall enjoy the right to a public trial was intended as a protection against star-chamber proceedings and to assure a check upon the conduct of courts. Trials are traditionally public, in other words, not because of the public's right to attend but because of a defendant's right to have the public present.

One way in which a committee proceeding may impinge disastrously on a later judicial proceeding was illustrated in the case of Daniel Delaney, a Collector of Internal Revenue. Delaney was indicted and charged with having accepted a bribe in connection with his duties as collector in Boston. While his trial was pending he was called before a congressional committee investigating suspected corruption in the Internal Revenue Service. His appearance before the committee received sensational publicity. In due course he was convicted in a Federal District Court, but

[7] Hearings before the Senate Special Committee to Investigate Organized Crime in Interstate Commerce, Part 7, pp. 877–78.

the conviction was set aside by the First Circuit Court of Appeals on the ground that the publicity engendered by the committee had precluded a fair trial, at least for the time being.

"This is not a case," Chief Judge Calvert Magruder said, "of pre-trial publicity of damaging material tending to indicate the guilt of a defendant, dug up by the initiative and private enterprise of newspapers. Here the United States, through its legislative department, by means of an open committee hearing held shortly before the trial of a pending indictment, caused and stimulated this massive pre-trial publicity on a nationwide scale." Judge Magruder went on to emphasize the striking disparities between a legislative trial and a judicial trial. "Some of this evidence," he said regarding the testimony publicized in the congressional hearing, "was indicative of guilt of the offenses charged in the indictment. Some of the damaging evidence would not be admissible at the forthcoming trial, because it related to alleged criminal derelictions and official misconduct outside the scope of the charges in the indictment. Not all the testimony of witnesses heard at the committee hearing ran the gauntlet of defense cross-examination. Nor was the published evidence tempered, challenged, or minimized by evidence offered by the accused." [8]

Pre-trial publicity of this kind must necessarily cast a shadow over subsequent judicial proceedings, and to a degree not easily evaluated. It commonly precludes a fair trial in the strict, old-fashioned sense of the term. The conditions which would be considered requisite to a fair trial in England do not obtain in the United States in the case of individuals indicted and prosecuted after prolonged and highly publicized appearances before congressional investigating committees. One cannot help wondering whether any person whose name has been publicized in a congressional hearing—who has been made the subject of defamatory headlines—can be subsequently tried in a manner which fully comports with the requirements of due process of law.

Sometimes procedures entirely appropriate to the function of a committee in exposing a general condition operate to take

[8] *Delaney* v. *U.S.*, 199 Fed. 2nd 107.

away from an individual rights that a court is bound to observe if he is brought before it for trial. The case of Charles E. Nelson and a number of associates, who were tried and convicted in a Federal District Court on the basis of evidence obtained by a Senate investigating committee, affords an interesting illustration of the point.

For a number of years before the Kefauver Committee began its probe into interstate crime, Nelson was widely known in the District of Columbia as a kingpin among gamblers. He appeared before the Kefauver Committee under subpoena and without counsel, and was questioned searchingly about his illegal gambling activities in the District. He was an evasive witness, and after a time the committee counsel suggested to the chairman that his attitude was contemptuous. The chairman admonished Nelson with some severity. "We are going to take a recess shortly," he said, "and I simply suggest that you think over carefully and come back when you resume the stand prepared to tell us the truth. Now is the chance, and it is up to you entirely. Do you understand what I say?"

Nelson came back after the recess with a refreshed memory and a relaxed tongue. He was asked a series of questions about his financial dealings, his bank accounts, tax returns, and his part in backing a numbers syndicate, and, specifically, about a "little red book" in which he had acknowledged that he kept his "ins" and "outs." He was asked whether he would permit a staff member to accompany him to his home and see the little red book. "It would be all right with me," he said.

At the conclusion of the hearing the acting chairman, Senator Lester C. Hunt of Wyoming, declared, "Mr. Nelson, we will have a staff member accompany you out to your home, and if you will turn over to him your account book, the little red book you speak of, he will see that you get a receipt for it, and the committee will return it to you at the very earliest date, so as not to inconvenience you any."

A staff member then accompanied Nelson to his home in Maryland and requested him to hand over the little red book. Saying that it was "not all together as yet," Nelson pulled out a drawer filled with other papers and books. The staff member, examining one of the books and finding it to be a 1942 ledger recording lotteries and numbers operations, asked Nelson if he could have the whole file. Nelson acquiesced, and the staff member took these papers back to Washington with him. The little red book was not among them. The committee subsequently turned these papers over to the United States Attorney. They constituted the principal evidence on which Nelson and his associates were indicted, tried, and convicted.

At his trial Nelson objected to the introduction of this evidence, charging that it had been obtained through violation of his rights under the Fourth and Fifth Amendments—that is, that it had been obtained under duress and therefore by what amounted to an illegal search and seizure. The trial court held, however, that Nelson had "voluntarily turned over" these papers to the committee, and so permitted them to be introduced as evidence against him.

The Circuit Court of Appeals, upon studying the trial record, came to the conclusion that Nelson's rights had been violated and that the evidence obtained by the staff member of the congressional committee should have been suppressed. "Nelson's freedom of choice," said Judge David Bazelon, "had been dissolved in a brooding omnipresence of compulsion. The committee threatened prosecution for contempt if he refused to answer, for perjury if he lied, and for gambling activities if he told the truth."

The elements of compulsion in this case were fairly formidable. Although the witness was presumably a man not easily intimidated, he might well have been overawed by the grip in which the committee held him. He was unaccompanied by counsel, and the committee did nothing to apprise him of rights which he might have asserted. Nobody told him that he would be allowed a lawyer if he wanted one, or that he could lawfully refuse to testify or to produce personal papers by pleading the privilege against self-incrimination. There seems ample warrant in this context for the Appellate Court's conclusion that Nelson's acquiescence in the investigator's demand for his papers was not "freely and intelligently given."

As Judge Bazelon pointed out: "If Nelson had been subjected to the same day-long pressures in a police station or a district attorney's office, his assent would not have been voluntary as a matter of law. . . . If there is anything to suggest that a congressional committee hearing is less awesome than a police station or a district attorney's office, and should therefore be viewed differently, it has escaped our notice. The similarity has become more apparent as the 'investigative' activities of Congress have become less distinguishable from the law-enforcement activities of the Executive."

The Nelson case helps to make clear how greatly the aims and interests of courts and committees differ. The tactics pursued by the committee in questioning Nelson and in wresting damaging admissions from him were undoubtedly of great utility in connection with the committee's efforts to expose the prevalence of gambling in and around the District of Columbia. They were not, however, defensible methods for bringing an individual gambler to justice. They turned an investigation into a legislative trial.

"The line between legitimate congressional inquiry and a trial of the individual may be difficult to draw with exactitude," Benjamin V. Cohen observed, "but that is no reason for ignoring and failing to observe any line. There is no excuse for congressional committees acting as 'people's courts' following the totalitarian patterns. Legislative trials, since the trial of Socrates, have had an odious history. Legislative trials combine the functions of prosecutor and judge and deny to the accused the right to impartial and independent judgment. Legislative trials are subject to the influence of partisanship, passion, and prejudice. Legislative trials are political trials. Let us remember that in the past legislative justice has tended to degenerate into mob injustice." [9]

[9] Address to the Indiana B'nai B'rith Convention, September 27, 1953.

III

The contemporary fervor for investigation has led committees of Congress into one additional form of encroachment on the judicial domain, which has taken the form of a direct challenge to the integrity and independence of the courts. One flagrant case in point occurred in California in June 1953. A House Judiciary subcommittee investigating income-tax scandals subpoenaed Federal District Judge Louis E. Goodman and sought to question him about certain grand-jury proceedings. The judge answered the subpoena, which he might legitimately have declined to do, but refused to submit to questioning. Instead he read to the subcommittee a letter signed by all seven federal district judges of California, expressing their united unwillingness to let any of their colleagues testify "with respect to any judicial proceedings." They explained what should have needed no explanation to a congressional body, that "the Constitution does not contemplate that such matters be reviewed by the legislative branch, but only by the courts."

Judge Goodman himself was courteous but resolute. He felt a duty, as an officer of the court, he declared, to maintain "the stability of our judicial process and the sanctity and secrecy of grand-jury proceedings." Only this kind of firm insistence upon the independence of a coordinate branch of the government can keep alive a political system based upon a separation of powers. Only this kind of respect for the integrity of its own characteristic function can preserve the independence of the individual branches. Only this kind of defense of its own jurisdiction by each of the branches can halt the ominous trend observed by Madison at the very inception of the Republic: "The legislative department is everywhere expanding its sphere of activity, and drawing all power into its impetuous vortex." [10]

---

[10] *The Federalist*, No. XLVIII.

CHAPTER V

LEGISLATIVE TRIALS

Those trained in the law know that we need not give up due process of law in order to save ourselves from internal dangers, any more than we need submit prisoners to the rack or to other forms of torture in order to solve crimes. We have the means and the ability to protect ourselves by fair standards of procedure. There is despair only when we turn to totalitarian techniques to defeat totalitarian forces.[1]

I

IN TIMES of tension, when men are convinced that the ideas of some of their fellow-men present a threat to the established order, the temptation is very great to deal with the heretics summarily and outside the law. The preservation of society—or to give it a more modern nomenclature, the maintenance of national security—has been the historic excuse for the auto-da-fé, for the star chamber, and for the kangaroo court. In the United States this temptation has found its most violent expression in lynch law and its most highly rationalized form in legislative trials.

The legislative trial is a device for condemning men without the formalities of due process. It has become the accepted means of dealing with persons suspected of Communist affiliations or of that even vaguer offense, Communist sympathies. Courts of law

[1] Justice William O. Douglas, Address before the American Law Institute, Washington, D.C., May 20, 1953.

are, in the view of zealots, slow, cumbersome, and uncertain instruments for this purpose. They have proved effective, it is true, in a limited sense: a number of Communist party leaders have been convicted and sent to prison under the Smith Act for participation in a conspiracy to advocate the duty and necessity of overthrowing the government of the United States by force and violence. There is no legal way to punish persons for the offense commonly called "disloyalty" or "fellow-traveling," but the legislative trial fills the gap admirably—from the zealots' point of view.

The legislative trial carries with it sanctions of a severe order. It is, to begin with, unimpeded by any statute of limitations; an error committed in the 1930s may be judged in the 1950s—and without any allowance whatever for altered conditions or a changed political climate. Defendants may be subjected to double or triple jeopardy, that is, they may be tried by different committees for the same deed. The punishments meted out are uninhibited by any sort of criminal code. Persons convicted in the courts of Congress may not suffer imprisonment, but they are likely to be subjected, in addition to loss of reputation, to a blacklisting which may effectively deny them any means of gaining a livelihood. Senator William E. Jenner was explicit as to his own view on this point in a speech he made in Springfield, Ohio, on April 29, 1954, and inserted in the *Congressional Record* of August 14, 1954:

> There is no place anywhere in American life for anyone who has ever collaborated with the Soviet fifth column for gain—whether it was Soviet gold, Communist votes, political office, fat business contracts, or moving-picture credits. There is no place even for innocents who scattered the Soviet word mines because the Soviet agents say they aren't loaded. . . .
> If they are foreigners, let us send them home. If they are American citizens, let us deprive them of the rights they despise. Let them earn their living as dishwashers or ditch diggers, but not in places where they can poison our minds.

There are no allowances here for youth or naïveté or good intentions—or even innocence—and there is no room for redemption. So far as intellectuals and professionals are concerned, it means a virtual exile to Siberia. Some of the committees seek to impose this kind of punishment through blacklists—among which the one compiled by the House Committee on Un-American Activities is the most formidable and voluminous—based upon mere identification with suspect groups and often upon uncorroborated allegations.

The legislative trial serves three distinct though related purposes: (1) it can be used to punish conduct which is not criminal; (2) it can be used to punish supposedly criminal conduct in the absence of evidence requisite to conviction in a court of law; and (3) it can be used to drive or trap persons suspected of "disloyalty" into committing some collateral crime such as perjury or contempt of Congress, which can then be subjected to punishment through a judicial proceeding. "It is hard to get them for their criminal activities in connection with espionage, but a way has been found," Senator McCarthy once remarked. "We are getting them for perjury and putting some of the worst of them away. For that reason I hope every witness who comes here is put under oath and his testimony is gone over with a fine-tooth comb, and if we cannot convict some of them for their disloyal activities, perhaps we can convict some of them for perjury." [2] That they may have been guilty of no violation of law in the first place seems of no concern to the Senator.

Legislative trials are now being used, deliberately and cynically, for each of the three purposes suggested above. The Durr case, the White case, and the Lattimore case, which are discussed in this chapter, illustrate each of the three, in order.

II

In March 1954 Senator James O. Eastland of Mississippi, acting as a one-man subcommittee of the Internal Security Subcommittee of the Senate Judiciary Committee, held hearings in

[2] Hearings before Senate Subcommittee on Foreign Relations (March 8, 1950), p. 14.

New Orleans for the ostensible purpose of exploring alleged Communist influence in the Southern Conference Educational Fund. The hearings served to pillory certain fellow-Southerners who had for many years, openly and ardently, opposed the Senator's "white supremacy" doctrines. The principal witness, or weapon, used to inflict this punishment was a man named Paul Crouch, who has made witnessing a career; he is one of those ex-Communists who, as Elmer Davis put it, "play the circuit of the congressional committees as horse players go from one track to another." [3] Crouch is a former officer of the Red Army, a former Soviet agent in the United States, having taken training for this service in Moscow, and a former convict, having served three years of a forty-year prison sentence for attempting to incite rebellion against the United States while he was a member of the Armed Forces.

His principal targets, by contrast, were Aubrey Williams, head of the National Youth Administration during the New Deal, president of the Southern Conference Educational Fund (the SCEF), and publisher of *The Southern Farm and Home;* Clifford Durr, a former member of the Federal Communications Commission, a former president of the National Lawyers Guild, and a former general counsel of the National Farmers Union; Virginia Durr, wife of Clifford Durr, a sister-in-law of Supreme Court Justice Hugo Black, and a militant champion of civil rights; Dr. James A. Dombrowski, executive director of the SCEF; and Myles Horton, a member of the SCEF and head of the Highlander Folk School, an interracial institution at Monteagle, Tennessee. All of them had long been outspoken advocates of racial equalitarianism in the South.

The manner in which these hearings were conducted was effectively reported in detail in the *Montgomery* (Alabama) *Advertiser*. The Durrs and Mr. Williams being residents of Montgomery, the *Advertiser* sent its assistant managing editor, Fred

[3] Elmer Davis, *But We Were Born Free* (Indianapolis: Bobbs-Merrill Co., 1954), p. 65.

Andersen, to New Orleans to cover the investigation. "Five grueling hours of grim charges and countercharges before a one-man Senate subcommittee," Andersen began his story after the first day's proceedings, "failed completely to label the Southern Conference Educational Fund as a Communist organization."

The hearings were conducted by Senator Eastland, to judge from Andersen's account of them, in an arrogant and overbearing manner. "Throughout the entire day," he reported, "the conduct of the hearing stirred repeated murmurs at the press table, where fourteen reporters labored under the glare of television klieg lights and back of a row of microphones and newsreel cameras." When Mrs. Durr's counsel, John P. Kohn of Montgomery, asked the chairman if he would be allowed to cross-examine witnesses who accused his client, Senator Eastland "frowned, and growled that he had 'no intention of standing still for heckling during this hearing; it is unheard of for a witness before a congressional committee to be cross-examined. It will not be done here.'

"When Kohn pressed for an idea of the 'ground rules' for the investigation, Eastland snapped, 'I will decide those as we go along and announce them when I desire. Sit down, sir. You are out of order.'"

The account of the first day ended somberly: "All day today, reporters at the press table could listen to the Eastland hearings and see out the window where an American flag fluttered gently."

The following day Eastland changed his mind about cross-examination and allowed Durr, as counsel for Williams, to interrogate Paul Crouch, Williams' accuser, because Williams "has shown every indication he wants to cooperate with the committee and has obviously answered each question to the best of his ability." But Durr almost at once found himself in the position of defendant. His questioning of Crouch was interrupted by the chief counsel of the subcommittee's subcommittee, Richard Arens, who asked Crouch, "Is Mr. Durr a Communist?"

Crouch responded characteristically, "I don't know if he still is or not."

"Was I a Communist?" Durr asked immediately.

"Yes, sir," replied Crouch, insisting that, although he had never met or talked to Durr, he had seen him "in various rented halls in Manhattan between 1938 and 1941."

"Name one," Durr demanded.

Crouch replied that it was "impossible to recall specific addresses," and he added that someone had told him Durr was a reliable Communist.

Durr then asked to take the witness stand himself, was sworn, and told the hearing, "Every word this man has said about me is an utter, complete, and absolute falsehood. We are both under oath. Therefore one or the other of us should be indicted for perjury."

Of Mrs. Durr, Crouch said, "I doubt very much she is or ever has been a Communist," but he accused her of "using her position as the sister-in-law of Justice Black to aid the cause of the Communist revolution"—specifically by helping to persuade the Justice and Mrs. Eleanor Roosevelt to speak at the organizational meeting of the Southern Conference for Human Welfare at Birmingham in 1938. Another subcommittee witness, John Butler, who identified himself as a former Communist, said Mrs. Durr had been a speaker at a labor-union meeting at Birmingham at one time, but acknowledged he had never seen her in any closed Communist meeting and that she had never been identified to him as a Communist.

Mrs. Durr said categorically, in response to questions by the sub-subcommittee counsel, that she was not and had never been a Communist or under Communist party discipline. But to all other questions she simply answered, on advice of her counsel, "I stand mute." Here was no Fifth Amendment plea but, rather, a candid, outright defiance, on principle, of the jurisdiction and authority of the sub-subcommittee.

Mrs. Durr had prepared a brief statement explaining her silence, but Senator Eastland would not permit her to make it in his presence or for the record. This is what Mrs. Durr wanted to say:

This hearing is no valid exercise of the investigatory powers of the United States Congress, but a kangaroo court where people, called as witnesses, are being tried as criminals—as traitors to their country, without any of the safeguards set up around such trials by the Constitution of the United States. They have been prejudged and condemned on the basis of testimony of paid informers, including an ex-convict, protected by congressional immunity and sheltered from cross-examination.

I wish to state for the record that I do not recognize the power of this committee to try me as a traitor. I refuse to accept its jurisdiction. If there are any valid charges against my patriotism, I demand a trial in open court with proper legal safeguards. I am asking for the rights that are the just due of any American citizen when his or her loyalty to their country has been impugned.

I do not plead the provisions of the Fifth Amendment against self-incrimination. I am not a Communist nor have I ever been. I only ask that I be accorded a fair trial in open court and not be subjected to the indignities and the disgrace of this public lynching of my life and reputation. I am invoking all other provisions of the Bill of Rights and of the Constitution which I believe are designed to protect citizens against outrages of this kind.

If the committee sees fit to pile into the record hearsay evidence, gossip, rumor, innuendos and suspicions, half-truths and lies concerning me, I am helpless to stop it, but I will not be a party to it. My life and my work are an open book. I have nothing to conceal and I have no apologies for anything I have done or said. This is not a proper body nor a proper forum to pass on my opinions, my friends, nor my acts, unless they have been against the laws of the United States.

I refuse to submit to the authority of this committee and I stand in total and utter contempt of it.

Dr. Dombrowski also rejected the protection of the Fifth Amendment, acknowledging association with a number of organizations which the sub-subcommittee counsel characterized as Communist fronts. He called Crouch "a liar" when that indefatigable accuser identified him as a former Communist. He gave full answers to questions put to him about himself and the SCEF but refused to give the names of any of the contributors to the organization, even under the threat of a contempt citation.[4]

Myles Horton, after asserting that the Fifth Amendment "was designed to protect people from inquisitorial proceedings such as these now being conducted by this very committee," said that he too would not invoke it. Then he went on:

> There are, however, some things that I cannot and will not do. I shall not and will not engage in any discussion before this committee with respect to my opinions on people or issues. I am not here as an expert witness holding myself out as qualified to give opinion evidence. I am here under subpoena. I have expressed my opinions and beliefs openly in the past and I shall continue to express them openly. But, as an American citizen, I believe that it is my right to express or withhold my opinions as I see fit, and to pick and choose the occasions when I will express them. I do not recognize the right of any public official or government body to require me to express them under the threat of punishment for failure to do so.
>
> Another thing I will not do is this. I will not talk about other people who are not here to protect themselves. These things I cannot do and be true to myself. I believe the provisions of the Constitution of the United States protect me in the position that I have taken and, except for the provision against self-incrimination, I invoke them all. . . .
>
> I believe that our Constitution protects me. If it does not, then the only court of final resort is my own conscience and I must be bound by its decisions. . . .
>
> If I had known of any acts of espionage or sabotage or any acts which threatened our national security, I would have immediately reported them to the proper authorities for action under our laws.
>
> The words "threat to the internal security of the United States" and "subversive activity" have become so vague, indefinite, and uncertain in meaning that it is possible for them to mean different things to different men. I know that within any intelligent definition of these words, nothing that I have ever done could possibly be viewed as dangerous to the security of my country or as a subversive activity, except by the most distorted of minds.
>
> I have acted upon the Christian postulation that all men are brothers

---

[4] Although these hearings were held in March 1954, they were not printed or published by the committee—at least up to December 15, 1954. Nor were any of the witnesses who refused to answer questions cited for contempt. All quotations in this section are taken from statements issued by the witnesses or from newspaper accounts of the proceedings.

and love freedom and that a democratic society is the only way of achieving freedom and brotherhood. These things I have taught, advocated, and lived, and will continue to preach. . . .

For this declaration Senator Eastland ordered him ejected from the room; marshals seized him and threw him out bodily.

The high point of the hearing, theatrically, came near the close, after all the accused persons had testified and when Crouch was recalled to the stand to recapitulate his allegations. To what he had said before he added the assertion that Mrs. Durr "had full knowledge of the Communist conspiracy" when she allegedly persuaded Justice Black to speak to the Southern Conference for Human Welfare in 1938. What followed was recounted by Andersen in the *Montgomery Advertiser*:

While Crouch was talking and obviously enjoying his first time to sit alone in the spotlight with the television cameras grinding away, Durr was gripping the rail of the jury box until his knuckles showed white.

Just before Crouch left the stand, Durr, in a voice shaking with emotion, told Jennings Perry, former editor of the *Nashville Tennessean*, who was sitting with him, "I'll kill that man."

As the admitted ex-Communist left the witness stand, Durr suddenly leaped around the edge of the jury box and began coming out of his coat.

Shaking with rage so he could hardly speak, the Montgomery attorney shouted at Crouch, "You son of a bitch—talk about my wife like that and I'll kill you."

Durr was forcibly restrained from assaulting Crouch by the brawny marshals. After he had made his attempt he collapsed and had to be taken to a hospital on account of a heart condition from which he had been suffering for some time. Perhaps violence—and contempt—were the only responses such a proceeding could evoke among Americans of honor and sensibility. Durr's conduct may have been quixotic, but it was in a tradition Americans have long respected. Mrs. Durr's refusal to answer questions may have been of dubious legal validity, but it surely had much moral justification.

None of the accused individuals haled before Senator Eastland had been indicted by a grand jury; none of them had even been charged with committing any crime. Most of the irrelevant hearsay and conjecture spewed out about them in the guise of "testimony" would not have been admissible in any court of law. The proceeding to which they were subjected was not an inquiry but a legislative trial—a trial with the manifest purpose of inflicting punishment by publicity. They had long since ceased to occupy any governmental positions; and the organization with which they were affiliated could not reasonably be considered a threat to the nation's internal security. They were pilloried by a committee of Congress because they had advocated ideas about racial equality displeasing to a particular senator.

Perhaps there was more genuine Americanism in defying this congressional committee than in complying with a procedure that did violence to American traditions of justice. Perhaps the "utter contempt" Virginia Durr expressed for it was all that Senator Eastland's sub-subcommittee deserved. Human freedom is dependent, in the last analysis, on just such contempt of arrogant and overbearing governmental authority.

At the conclusion of the three-day hearing Andersen took a press-table poll of the nine reporters who had sat through the entire course of the investigation. He asked the same question of each one: "On the basis of what you have seen and heard here, who of the principals represents the greatest threat to American ideals?"

There were four votes for Senator Eastland, two for Paul Crouch, one for Dr. Dombrowski, one for a Miami contractor, Max Shlafrock, who had sought refuge in the Fifth Amendment, and one for Richard Arens, the sub-subcommittee's chief counsel.

III

There is a portion of the Fifth Amendment—its very opening words, indeed—rarely cited and commonly ignored in congressional investigations: "No person shall be held to answer for a capital, or otherwise infamous crime, unless on a presentment or indictment of a grand jury. . . ." In contemporary congressional investigations persons are frequently "held to answer" for infamous crimes respecting which a grand jury has *declined* to furnish a presentment or indictment. This practice is an outright perversion of the constitutional injunction.

A whole catalogue of cases was provided by Attorney General Herbert Brownell, Jr., in his testimony before the Senate Internal Security Subcommittee under William E. Jenner of Indiana on November 17, 1953. A few days prior to this appearance the Attorney General made a speech to the Executives Club in Chicago in which he asserted that "Harry Dexter White was known to be a Communist spy by the very people who appointed him to the most sensitive and important position he ever held in the government." In his appearance before the Jenner Subcommittee—an extraordinarily dramatic appearance widely covered by radio and television and motion-picture cameras—Brownell reiterated the assertion that White was a wartime spy. "Of course, no one could, with any validity, suggest today," he said, "that there is any doubt that White was in this espionage ring."

In the course of the same hearing the Attorney General declassified and read aloud to the subcommittee (and also, of course, to the television audience) two letters sent by the director of the Federal Bureau of Investigation to the military aide to the President—one of them marked "Top Secret," the other marked "Personal and Confidential"; and he summarized in considerable detail the contents of an FBI report sent to the White House in 1946.

Not only White but a number of other former government employees were named in the letters and the report as members of two Soviet espionage rings. In the light of these disclosures a statement made by the Attorney General at the outset of his testimony seems perplexing: "I fully realize these grave responsibilities which I have as chief law-enforcement officer of this nation not to use confidential reports in my possession to disclose charges against individuals except through established court procedures. Those of us in the Department of Justice will never violate that basic concept of our American jurisprudence."

"But the White case," Brownell went on, "of course, is not that situation. The basic facts of the two spy rings which existed in the government at that time have been fully exposed in court and before congressional committees. This subcommittee recently published a very excellent report documenting those facts."

Then why, one wonders, did the Attorney General think it proper or necessary to retell this twice-told tale? The Department of Justice had presented the case against Harry White to a grand jury in 1947, presumably setting before it all the pertinent and admissible information contained in the FBI report of 1946. The grand jury had not returned an indictment.

Brownell offered the subcommittee an explanation for the grand jury's failure to indict. The explanation was that when White came before the grand jury, much of the "evidence" against him had been gleaned by tapping his telephone conversations. Wiretaps were not admissible as evidence in federal courts. And in addition, he pointed out, the government had not had available to it at that time certain documents in White's handwriting subsequently discovered (after White's death) among Whittaker Chambers' notorious "pumpkin papers." However, the Attorney General, having divulged what he said was their import, did not make the wiretap records themselves available for examination. Nor did he present any evidence to prove that White himself had given the documents to Chambers—obviously an essential link in the chain of evidence necessary to convict White of espionage. The documents may have been stolen from White or passed by him innocently to someone who gave them to Chambers, despite Chambers' contention to the contrary. One of the essential characteristics of espionage, of course, is an intent to aid a foreign government or to injure the United States—or at least reason to believe that the information communicated will have one of these results.

Harry White, who died in 1948, was not at hand to defend himself. Before his death he had unequivocally denied under oath all the charges made against him by the Attorney General in 1953. He had done this not only privately before the grand jury but also publicly before the House Committee on Un-American Activities.

Some of the living persons accused of espionage by the Attorney General had also denied the accusation under oath—steadfastly, forthrightly, and redundantly—although a number of others had refused to answer questions, availing themselves of the Fifth Amendment's privilege against self-incrimination. If they were, in fact, spies, their crime, having been committed while the United States was at war, entailed a death penalty and therefore was subject to no statute of limitations. If they were, in fact, spies, those who denied it were guilty of perjury in addition to espionage. Why, then, were they not tried on either count in a court of law? The answer seems inescapable: because there was not sufficient evidence to convict them in a court of law.

When the grand jury of 1947 failed to indict a single one of the thirty-odd government employees or former government employees accused of espionage by Elizabeth Bentley, a frequent witness before investigating committees and an undercover informant for the FBI, the House Committee on Un-American Activities undertook to punish by publicity presumed offenses which could not be punished by due process of law. The pretext on which the committee took jurisdiction in this matter was that it desired to investigate the broad general problem of espionage in the government with a view to recommending remedial legislation. But its conduct was not altogether dissimilar to that of a posse, which, convinced that a court will not convict someone it suspects of having committed rape, decides to take the law into its own hands and administer a punishment it believes to be deserved. By the time the Jenner Subcommittee undertook to "retry" these cases in 1953, the pretext of investigating wartime espionage had become pretty diaphanous—so diaphanous, indeed, as to reveal the naked outlines of a partisan political purpose.

The persons condemned as spies by the Attorney General may

have been guilty, but the mere accusation of a prosecutor does not establish guilt, except in totalitarian societies such as the Soviet Union. Brownell offered no evidence in support of his accusations beyond the evidence unsuccessfully offered to the grand jury. He merely asserted that FBI reports, based for the most part on unidentified informants and on illegal wiretapping, proved them guilty. But although he displayed no hesitancy about disclosing what he asserted to be the purport of the wiretaps and of the anonymous information contained in the FBI reports, he conspicuously failed to make public the reports themselves; the country, in short, was simply asked to take his word for it that those he condemned were guilty.

Americans, however, are not accustomed to taking the word of Attorneys General in such matters—even when it is backed up by the formidable authority of the FBI. The courts were functioning at the time. The normal processes of justice were available to test these cases. There was no justification for imitating totalitarian methods and substituting a legislative trial for due process of law.

Without doubt any court would have said to the Attorney General that if he wished to prosecute he must present evidence to support his charges. When the Department of Justice charged Judith Coplon in 1949 with having tried to transmit to a Soviet agent certain data slips or abstracts culled from confidential files of the FBI, it balked at disclosing the material from which she had allegedly gleaned her information. Disclosure of these FBI data, said the Department, would imperil national security. But Federal Judge Albert Reeves, who conducted the first Coplon trial, declared firmly that the government would have to decide whether national security could best be served by convicting the defendant or preserving the secrecy of FBI files; it could not do both. "I regretfully have to state," said Judge Reeves, "that a judge is charged with a responsibility—to see that justice is done. If it turns out that the government has come into court exposing itself, then it will have to take the peril. If it embarrasses the government to disclose relevant material, then the government ought not to be here."

Something of the same sort might have been said to Attorney General Brownell when, before the Jenner Subcommittee, he charged men with espionage but withheld the proof of his charges on the plea of national security. He might have been told, in a homely American phrase, to put up or shut up. He might have been told, and should have been told, that national security depends less upon the public condemnation of suspected individuals than upon maintenance of the great principles embodied in the concept "due process of law."

A legislative trial served here as an easy short cut—a device more urbane yet no less repugnant to traditions of fair play than lynch law. It may well have inflicted upon the national security it pretended to protect a wound deeper and more dangerous by far than any that could have been inflicted by the persons whom the Attorney General condemned as spies—without indictment, without published evidence, without trial, and without due process of law.

IV

"No man has ever been more relentlessly persecuted by a congressional committee," said Elmer Davis, "than Owen Lattimore by the Internal Security Committee under Senator McCarran." [5] Mr. Davis's superlative, even in so highly competitive an area, is unlikely to be successfully challenged. Lattimore was selected as a scapegoat by the China Lobby—that frenzied group which views China as an American province treasonably turned over to the Communists.

Until 1950 Owen Lattimore, director of the Walter Hines Page School of International Relations at The Johns Hopkins University, though distinguished among Far Eastern scholars, enjoyed no great general renown. As a businessman and journalist who had

[5] Davis, op. cit., p. 65.

lived and traveled widely in China and Central Asia, he acquired a knowledge of the history, geography, culture, dialects, and nascent nationalism of China that was extraordinary if not unique among Westerners. His interest focused, in time, upon the little-known areas of inner Asia—upon Mongolia in particular—and he became the outstanding interpreter of this region, writing of it not only in scholarly papers but also in books and magazine articles intended for more general consumption. Because what he wrote was readable, it has sometimes been disparaged as unscholarly by his detractors; but among experts the world over, his *Inner Asian Frontiers of China*—to cite only what appears to be the most highly regarded among his several books—is generally considered scholarship of the highest order and an invaluable contribution to Western understanding of the Far East.

Lattimore served from 1934 to 1941 as editor of the magazine *Pacific Affairs,* published under the auspices of the Institute of Pacific Relations. During World War II he was deputy director of Pacific Operations of the Office of War Information and acted for a time, by designation of President Roosevelt, as political adviser to Generalissimo Chiang Kai-shek. These undertakings were apparently responsible for the disfavor into which he fell among the China Lobbyists.

Lattimore was suddenly catapulted into notoriety when Senator McCarthy, hard pressed to substantiate his various charges of Communist infiltration into the State Department, named him (although he had never been employed in the Department and was at the time chief of a United Nations mission in Afghanistan) as "one of the top Communist agents in this country." A Senate Foreign Relations subcommittee under the chairmanship of Millard Tydings of Maryland was created to investigate the McCarthy charges. It conducted extensive hearings, listened to McCarthy and to several ex-Communist witnesses who supported him, interrogated Lattimore at length, and came to the conclusion that the charges amounted to no more than a "fraud and a hoax perpetrated on the Senate of the United States and the American people." [6]

But there is never a final clearance from a McCarthy charge. Senator Tydings was defeated for re-election in the fall of 1950, and his defeat was joyously interpreted by McCarthy and certain of his senatorial allies as overturning the findings of the Tydings Subcommittee. In July 1951 the Senate Judiciary Committee's Internal Security Subcommittee under Senator McCarran began a new inquiry, centered this time on the Institute of Pacific Relations (the IPR) but with Lattimore as a principal target.

The subcommittee's investigation began sensationally with a raid on a barn located on the grounds of the country home of the Institute's chief administrative officer. Old correspondence and documents of the IPR stored there had been previously examined by FBI agents, who apparently had found nothing incriminating among them. But now subcommittee staff members scooped them up, transported them under armed convoy to Washington, and for five months ransacked them. Having armed itself in this way, the subcommittee summoned Lattimore and questioned him in a single executive session. This was followed by six months of public hearings in which a number of witnesses, including several who had previously appeared before the Tydings Subcommittee, were allowed to hurl charges at Lattimore and the IPR under the comfortable cover of congressional immunity.

The bitter hostility of the subcommittee, and especially of Senator McCarran, toward Lattimore is difficult to understand or explain. Perhaps it grew out of the fact that Lattimore had reacted to the charges against him with indignation and had struck back at his accusers lustily and irreverently. In *Ordeal by Slander*, published in 1950, he treated with blistering scorn the kind of so-called anti-communism that equates liberalism with disloyalty and ignores all the traditional American concepts of decency and fair play. By the time he was at last allowed to

[6] Report of the Senate Committee on Foreign Relations, July 20, 1950, p. 167.

come before the McCarran Subcommittee and refute in public the accusations that had been made against him publicly, he came with a prepared statement that expressed a long-pent-up anger and a rankling sense of injustice. It was not a mild statement, not even, perhaps, a mannerly one. A softer answer might have been more politic. But it is doubtful, in view of the subcommittee's evident animus, that even the softest of answers could have turned away its wrath. In any case, some tolerance was due a man who had been forced to wait helplessly for many months while his good name as a scholar and a citizen was being impugned.

Lattimore came before the subcommittee on February 26, 1952. Chairman McCarran opened the proceedings with a preliminary statement that withdrew even the pretense of impartiality. Criticism of the committee, he made clear, was indistinguishable in his mind from communism:

Every Communist in America has taken opportunity to cast invective and discouraging and disparaging remarks with reference to this committee and its membership. We were fully advised before we undertook this task that such would be the course and procedure. It is not at all out of line with the general procedure of the Communist party and Communists generally in the world. . . . A statement has been filed today by the witness. The ticker shortly after noon announced that that statement was available to those who saw fit to read it and it was at the office of the attorney for the witness. The press has that statement now. Of course, that statement and its remarks are no longer privileged, as that term is known in the law. The witness must be responsible for the full gravity of his remarks produced in that statement. In that statement there is carried out the same policy as has been carried out against this committee. Intemperate and provocative expressions are there set out and elaborated upon. . . .[7]

With this introduction began a legislative trial unparalleled in American history. For twelve days Owen Lattimore was kept continuously on the witness stand—a record of its kind—and was not so much interrogated as relentlessly baited and harassed by in-

[7] Hearings on the Institute of Pacific Relations before the Senate Internal Security Subcommittee (February 26, 1952), Part 9, pp. 2897–98.

quisitors relieving each other in relays—the counsel of the Judiciary Committee and the counsel of the Internal Security Subcommittee and the seven subcommittee members. There was not a voice friendly to Lattimore, nor even a dispassionate one, to be heard in that curious courtroom. Lattimore himself was consistently kept from making a coherent defense. His counsel, Abe Fortas, was silenced at the very outset.

Before Lattimore began his statement Fortas addressed the chair as follows: "Senator, I should like to ask you to advise me of the rights and privileges of attorneys. I have examined your record of these hearings and I find that you yourself made the following statement on July 25, 1951—"

THE CHAIRMAN: What I said is not necessary. I can tell you in a minute, Mr. Fortas.

I did tell you privately and I will tell you now on the record that you will be permitted to remain here. You will not be permitted to testify and you will not be permitted to suggest answers to questions. When the witness seeks your counsel he will have opportunity to obtain your counsel.

MR. FORTAS: Thank you, Senator. May I ask whether I am permitted to object to questions?

THE CHAIRMAN: No, sir.

In this atmosphere and under these auspices, Owen Lattimore began his statement. He completed one sentence and was interrupted to identify an exchange of letters between himself and the subcommittee chairman. Then he was invited to proceed.

"The impression has been assiduously conveyed in your proceedings—" the witness began again. He got no further.

"Do you mean by 'assiduously conveyed,'" the counsel of the Judiciary Committee, Jay G. Sourwine, broke in, "to make the charge that the committee has intended to convey a certain impression?"

"I mean," said Lattimore, "that witness after witness before this committee has attempted to convey this impression and that no witnesses have been asked any question that might test their veracity."

MR. SOURWINE: Do you mean to charge, sir, that the committee has intended to convey a particular impression?

MR. LATTIMORE: I cannot answer for what is in the minds of the committee.

MR. SOURWINE: We are asking you what is in your mind, sir, what you intended to convey by the use of that phrase.

MR. LATTIMORE: I intended to convey by the use of that phrase exactly what is stated here.

Senator Homer Ferguson of Michigan, a member of the subcommittee, broke in at this point with a question manifestly rhetorical. He was followed by Senator Arthur V. Watkins of Utah, another member. Then Sourwine again: "If we might get back to this question of your phrase, 'assiduously conveyed,' what did you mean by that word 'assiduously'?"

"Well," Lattimore responded, "I believe the Latin etymology of the word probably means to sit down and stick at."

"It comes from *assiduus*, doesn't it?" queried Sourwine. "Did you use it in that sense?"

"That is the sense in which I used it," said Lattimore, somewhat dryly.

"Go ahead, sir," said Sourwine.

So Lattimore had another try at reading the prepared statement he had waited so long to deliver. "The impression has been assiduously conveyed in your proceedings," he read, "that I am a Communist or a Communist sympathizer or dupe—" The round of questions began again.

MR. SOURWINE: How has that been conveyed, Mr. Lattimore?

MR. LATTIMORE: Well, the record is full of it, sir.

MR. SOURWINE: You are making the charge, sir, and has anyone on the committee conveyed that impression, or has it been conveyed only by witnesses testifying here under oath?

MR. LATTIMORE: I think some of the leading questions of members of the committee could be so interpreted, perhaps.

MR. SOURWINE: Are you interpreting the questions asked by the committee as intended to convey that you were a Communist or Communist sympathizer or dupe?

MR. LATTIMORE: In writing this opening part of my statement, I was trying to convey an over-all impression of hearings that had been going on for eight months or so, in which hostile evidence, evidence hostile to me and others, has been piled up, and at this present time I am attempting to deal with that accumulation of many months.

Then Senator Ferguson came in with a succession of questions as to whether the witness considered it important "to inquire as to whether or not an institution that is giving information to the public has been penetrated by Communists or Communist sympathizers." After a good deal of this, Lattimore was again told to proceed with his statement.

"The impression has been assiduously conveyed in your proceedings," he began, "that I am a Communist or a Communist sympathizer or dupe; that I master-minded the Institute of Pacific Relations—"

This short additional phrase touched off another interruption by Sourwine and a lengthy set of questions regarding the influence, if any, of the Institute of Pacific Relations upon the Far Eastern experts of the State Department. Chairman McCarran and Senator O'Conor joined Senator Ferguson and the committee counsel in this diversion. After interrogation and responses covering sixteen pages of the printed record, Senator Herbert R. O'Conor of Maryland, who had assumed the chair, said, "Mr. Lattimore, you may continue your statement. I think you were just at the latter part of the second paragraph on the first page."

"I am still in the first part of the second paragraph," Mr. Lattimore said, "so if I may resume so that readers will not lose track of the sense—"

SENATOR O'CONOR: You have been over the first part three or four times, the "assiduously conveyed."

MR. LATTIMORE: But the sentence hasn't been finished yet.

SENATOR O'CONOR: You would prefer to go back and continue that? I wonder whether we could withhold our questioning until the whole paragraph is read?

MR. LATTIMORE: That would accord with my interest in the subject, Senator.

And so the witness completed his sentence. Indeed, he even completed a second sentence before he was again interrupted.

The impression has been assiduously conveyed in your proceedings that I am a Communist or a Communist sympathizer or dupe; that I master-minded the Institute of Pacific Relations; that the Institute of Pacific Relations and I master-minded the Far Eastern experts of the State Department; and that the State Department "sold" China to the Russians. Every one of these is false—utterly and completely false.

The subcommittee was determined, it was plain, to keep Lattimore from making any coherent statement. It was determined to cut off any effective refutation of the charges that had been made against him. There was no semblance of inquiry in this proceeding, no search for information, no disposition to alter or modify entrenched prejudices. One after another, the members of the subcommittee and its two counsels jabbed questions at the witness, designed only, it seemed, to disconcert him, to interrupt the flow of his testimony, to provoke him into intemperance and extravagance of expression, and, finally, to lead or trap him into errors of recollection or misstatements of fact that could be used subsequently as a basis for charging him with deliberate falsification.

The progress of this proceeding was watched by at least one member of the press with growing revulsion. The hearing conjured up images of ancient inquisitorial techniques and of the mental bludgeoning which is said to be the typical Soviet police method of eliciting information. But information was not the aim of this inquiry. It was hard to regard its aim as anything but sadistic.

Repeatedly Lattimore was pressed to give categorical answers to questions which, in his own judgment, could be answered properly only with qualifications and elaboration. Often the questions were couched in such a way as to put words into his mouth. One extended colloquy between him and Senator Ferguson may serve to illustrate the point:

SENATOR FERGUSON: How many divisions or armies did Chiang Kai-shek have to put on his border up at the Communist border to preserve the integrity of his rule?

MR. LATTIMORE: I don't recall the figure, Senator, but I do recall that in the opinion of some of the American diplomatic and military representatives in China, some of those troops were being unnecessarily immobilized.

SENATOR FERGUSON: That was not my question. My question was, how many did he use on the border?

MR. LATTIMORE: I don't know.

SENATOR FERGUSON: Did he use any?

MR. LATTIMORE: There were troops at the corner of northwest China where Chiang Kai-shek's free China and the Communist-held part of China joined.

SENATOR FERGUSON: But it is your contention now that they were not there to keep the Communists from moving into the Nationalist territory?

MR. LATTIMORE: No; it is my contention that many of the Americans in the field at the time considered that the blockade of the Communists was unnecessarily large and severe, immobilized an unnecessarily large number of Chiang's troops.

SENATOR FERGUSON: But they did immobilize some of his troops?

MR. LATTIMORE: That is right.

SENATOR FERGUSON: And at the very time that at least Chiang Kai-shek felt that it was necessary to preserve his own army to keep the Communists back, you were advocating arms and supplies and munitions to the Communists?

MR. LATTIMORE: No, sir; you are talking about two different situations.

SENATOR FERGUSON: Please do not tell me what I am talking about. I am just asking you the question.

MR. LATTIMORE: Well, in my opinion, then, Senator, there were two different situations. One was during the period when the United States had no access and no hope of immediate access to the coast of China.

The second was the period when we were rapidly approaching the coast of China and when many people thought, as was discussed in the press at the time, I remember, that the Japanese would withdraw from the home islands of Japan and make a last stand in Manchuria, in which case the question of combined American-Chinese operations on the mainland against Manchuria would have been very important.

SENATOR FERGUSON: All right. Now let us go back to the question I was asking.

In June of 1945, was it not true that Chiang Kai-shek had immobilized some of his troops against Japan and in order that he may protect his army from the Chinese Communist Army?

MR. LATTIMORE: It is true, Senator, that he had immobilized part of his army. It is also true that in the opinion of many American observers there at the time it was unnecessary.

SENATOR FERGUSON: Mr. Lattimore, we are not going to get through today unless we can get the answers to these questions. I can stay over here as long as you can stay over there.

MR. ARNOLD [Thurman Arnold, then serving as counsel to Mr. Lattimore]: Mr. Chairman, he is answering.

THE CHAIRMAN: Just a minute, Counsel. I told the counsel when he first commenced this hearing as to what their limitations were. When he wants advice, he can ask you for advice. You will not participate in the proceedings.

MR. ARNOLD: I am sorry, Senator. He permitted me to read the answer to the question before, and I thought I could be helpful in the proceedings by merely striking out the last part of that answer.

SENATOR FERGUSON: That is what I think ought to be stricken out, and if he will just stick to the answers he and I will get along.

THE CHAIRMAN: You just tell the witness to answer the question, and you will give him some pretty good advice.

MR. ARNOLD: I think he is trying, Senator.

MR. LATTIMORE: I think the trouble here, Senator Ferguson, is merely that—

SENATOR FERGUSON: Are you answering my question?

MR. LATTIMORE: Yes.

SENATOR FERGUSON: All right.

MR. LATTIMORE: I cannot accept your statement of the question as if it were my opinion on the question.

SENATOR FERGUSON: It was a fact, therefore you would have to know. Did you or did you not know whether or not Chiang Kai-shek was demobilizing or, as you called it that, part of his troops between his part of China and the Communist part of China, to protect his part of China from the Communists?

MR. LATTIMORE: I knew that he was immobilizing part of his troops in that area, and I also knew that many Americans in China considered that he was immobilizing in excessive number.

THE CHAIRMAN: That is no part of the answer. That is another part.

SENATOR FERGUSON: Thank you, Mr. Chairman. That was in June 1945?

MR. LATTIMORE: Generally speaking, in that period; yes.

SENATOR FERGUSON: Yes. And that was the very time that you were advocating Mr. Lamont, over his signature, to advocate that we furnish to the Communists in China munitions and arms. You can answer that question "Yes" or "No."

MR. LATTIMORE: I don't think that question is susceptible to a "Yes" or "No" answer, Senator.

THE CHAIRMAN: Do you want to answer it "Yes" or "No" or not answer it? Just say whether you do or do not.

MR. LATTIMORE: No; I don't want to answer it "Yes" or "No."

SENATOR FERGUSON: Then I will take it for granted that the two documents speak for themselves, the answer before and the documents.

MR. LATTIMORE: I should like to explain, Senator, that I am referring to a new situation, not an old one.

THE CHAIRMAN: If you say you cannot answer the question, there is no explanation, if you cannot answer it "Yes" or "No." If you cannot answer it, you cannot answer it.

MR. LATTIMORE: May I not explain why I can't answer it, Senator?

SENATOR FERGUSON: No; I did not ask you that question, to explain why.[8]

Over and over again, counsel and members of the committee, having studied the IPR's ancient files without making them available to the witness, asked questions about incidents that had occurred a decade earlier. The characteristic method of questioning was to demand a categorical answer from Lattimore about matters which in his mind were hazy or forgotten and then to produce some documentary indication that the answer had been in error. "I would like to explain, Mr. Chairman," said Lattimore at one point, when he had confessed inability to recall whether, when he was in Tokyo in 1945, he had known several Japanese whose names were reeled off in rapid succession by Mr. Sourwine, "a number of times in these hearings the names of people have been mentioned whom I totally failed to recall, and later on some memorandum or other document is brought out which indicated that I did meet them. This is part of the whole procedure, which I should very respectfully like to criticize."

"That part will be stricken from the record," the chairman responded. "You are not here for the purpose of criticizing; you are here for the purpose of testifying under oath, and you are under oath."[9]

Lattimore found himself caught in a vise, one jaw of which

[8] Ibid. (March 10, 1952), Part 10, pp. 3392–94.
[9] Ibid., p. 3298.

was formed by the committee's detailed knowledge of the IPR files, the other jaw by its insistence that he discuss with crisp definiteness incidents which had occurred long before and were vague in his memory. The committee deliberately, systematically, tightened this vise until it had succeeded in eliciting a small series of discrepancies that could be represented as a basis for a perjury indictment and prosecution. This was not inquiry designed to inform the Congress or enlighten the public. It was inquiry designed to punish an individual by provoking him into errors that could be called criminal. It would be difficult to discover anywhere a more shameful prostitution of the congressional investigating power.

Here is one example of the way in which the committee developed a conflict between testimony and the records in its possession—testimony based on recollection of ancient incidents, the records conned secretly by the questioners and withheld from the witness. When Lattimore appeared before the McCarran Subcommittee in executive session he testified about a meeting with the Soviet Ambassador to Washington, Constantin Oumansky, which took place, he said, "just before I went out to Chungking as the Generalissimo's adviser, when Mr. Carter invited Mr. Oumansky and me to have dinner with him in a hotel here in Washington." Asked by counsel Robert Morris to fix the date of this meeting, Lattimore said, "It was just before I went to China, so it must have been June or early July of 1941."

"That was therefore after the Hitler invasion of the Soviet?" Mr. Morris then asked.

"Yes," said Lattimore.

Eight months later, in the course of the public hearing, Morris asked Lattimore, "Did you testify that your meeting with Mr. Oumansky was after the Hitler invasion of the Soviet Union?"

Lattimore responded, "Yes, I believe I did. I couldn't guarantee that, just to the best of my recollection."

Morris then introduced a letter from the IPR files dated June 20, 1941, addressed to Owen Lattimore, with the typed signature of Edward C. Carter, and another letter from Carter to Philip

Jessup, dated June 23, 1941, both referring to a luncheon "last Wednesday" with Mr. Oumansky. Lattimore said at once, "Mr. Chairman, may I point out that this letter establishes the fact that my recollection was wrong in believing that I had that lunch with Mr. Carter and Oumansky in Washington after the Hitler invasion of Russia. It seems to have taken place before." [10] "The Hitler invasion of the Soviet" occurred on June 22, 1941. The Lattimore luncheon with Oumansky evidently occurred on June 18, 1941.

On the basis of this testimony Lattimore was charged with perjury "in that the luncheon conference between him and the Soviet Ambassador was held while the Hitler-Stalin Pact was still in effect, and before the Hitler invasion of the Soviet Union on June 22, 1941."

Perjury under the Code of the District of Columbia is a crime committed when a defendant, having properly taken an oath or made an affirmation, "willfully and contrary to such oath or affirmation states or subscribes any material matter which he does not believe to be true." [11] Lattimore's misstatement seems to meet none of these conditions. So far from being made willfully —that is, with an intent to deceive the subcommittee—it appears to have been made casually and in response to a suggestion offered by counsel; it is not too much, indeed, to say that the significant words of the misstatement were formulated by Morris. It was the subcommittee's counsel who said, "That was therefore after the Hitler invasion of the Soviet?" The witness merely answered "Yes" respecting a matter to which he attached no significance.

That a man should err by four days in fixing the date of a luncheon that had taken place a full decade earlier hardly seems surprising; moreover, the error was readily and candidly corrected as soon as it was called to the witness's attention. There is no indication here that he was trying to mislead or deceive the subcommittee either at the executive session or at the open hearing.

[10] Ibid., p. 3265.
[11] 22 D.C. Code, 2501.

Instead, every indication suggests that he was honestly confused as to whether the luncheon took place before or after the invasion of Russia.

In due course the McCarran Subcommittee turned its record over to the Department of Justice and asked that Department to prosecute Lattimore for perjury. When the Department seemed to be lagging in compliance, Senator McCarran prodded it pointedly. On December 16, 1952, Lattimore was indicted on seven counts of perjury alleged to have been committed before the subcommittee.

When the case came before Federal District Judge Luther W. Youngdahl, Lattimore's lawyers filed motions to dismiss the indictment in its entirety. The judge, dismissing four of the seven charges, had this to say in his opinion:

> Apparently the committee could discover no evidence from its investigation or the testimony of the various witnesses that the defendant lied in denying that he was a Communist, a member of the Communist party, a Soviet spy, or a fellow-traveler. . . . In the indictment under consideration, defendant is not charged with lying in denying that he was a Communist or a member of the Communist party. The judgment here charges defendant with committing perjury as to his sympathies with communism or Communist interests (count one); whether he had been told or knew certain persons were Communists (counts two and three); whether he had published certain articles in *Pacific Affairs* by Communists (count four); whether he had a luncheon engagement with Soviet Ambassador Oumansky in July 1941 after the Hitler invasion (count five); that he did not at the request of Lauchlin Currie take care of his mail at the White House (count six); and whether he had made prearrangements with the Communist party to get in Yenan (count seven).
>
> It appears from the record and the hearings of the committee that the charges reflected in the seven counts in the indictment related to a period of fifteen to twenty years before the hearings. . . .
>
> Aside from the reasons of invalidity as to certain counts as hereinafter expressed, there is serious doubt in the court's mind whether any count in this indictment can finally pass the test of materiality.

The first count of the indictment—one of the most remarkable counts ever introduced into a United States court—was set aside by Judge Youngdahl as "fatally defective." It arose from a portion of Lattimore's formal statement to the McCarran Subcommittee—the statement he had so much difficulty in delivering. He sought, voluntarily, to make his political position altogether clear to the subcommittee, flinging down a gauntlet to all his accusers. And so he said sweepingly:

All kinds of attempts have been made to depict me as a Communist or a Soviet agent. I have in fact been falsely identified as a fellow-traveler, sympathizer, or follower of the Communist line or promoter of Communist interests. Now I want to make my position clear. I am not interested in graduations or degrees of disloyalty. I have no use for fancy, legalistic distinctions. I am none of these things and have never been. I am not and have never been a Communist, a Soviet agent, a sympathizer, or any other kind of promoter of communism or Communist interests, and all of these are nonsense. I so testified long ago, under oath, before the Tydings Subcommittee, and I do so again.[12]

It can hardly be said that there was anything evasive or fuzzy or even guarded about this statement. It threw the lie at witnesses such as Louis Budenz, who had dredged up a recollection that he had heard Lattimore referred to as a trusted Communist affiliate. It categorically denied that he was or ever had been a Soviet agent, a member of the Communist party, or a fellow-traveler. But though the McCarran Subcommittee did not scruple, in its report, to call Lattimore "a conscious, articulate instrument of the Soviet conspiracy," the Department of Justice did not prosecute him for his denial of this allegation. It did not prosecute him for his denial of any acts or affiliations capable of objective proof; perjury could have been shown respecting these denials if it could have been proved that he had been a member of the Communist party or that he had committed espionage or sabotage or subversion in behalf of the Soviet government. Instead, the Department of Justice charged him with perjury merely on the basis of his denial that he had ever been "a sympathizer or any other kind of promoter of communism or Communist interests."

The ambiguity of the terms employed in this charge makes it

[12] Ibid., p. 2947.

very nearly meaningless. What constitutes a "sympathizer"? What degree of tolerance for Russian or Chinese or Yugoslav or classical Marxist communism or Trotskyism reaches the level of sympathy? What overt acts amount to "promoting" Communist interests? Indeed, what are "Communist interests"? As Lattimore's lawyers asked in their brief in his behalf, "Did President Roosevelt promote Communist interests when he furnished lend-lease to Russia? Did General Marshall promote Communist interests when he criticized Chiang Kai-shek's government?" Of course there are those who believe they did. But if a man can be charged with perjury for denying that such conduct made him a sympathizer with or a promoter of communism, then no man whose views or acts happened transiently to coincide with the party line or with Soviet policy would be immune from indictment.

Lattimore's assertion, which the indictment alleges to be false, was that he had never been prompted to act or write or speak by any sympathy for communism or by any intent to promote Communist interests. This is an assertion that cannot be disproved by showing a parallelism between some of Lattimore's opinions and some of the Soviet government's statements. If the assertion was false, the falsity is not susceptible of objective proof. Perhaps it could be shown that he felt sympathy for ideas that Senator McCarran considered communistic or promoted interests that Senator Jenner identified with communism—but these are matters Lattimore never denied.

Judge Youngdahl compellingly condemned the main charge against Lattimore in his opinion striking it down. He said:

First, this count is violative of the Sixth Amendment, which protects the accused in the right to be informed of the nature and cause of the accusation against him. . . .

Defendant in the first count is charged with lying in denying that he was a sympathizer or promoter of Communist interests. It seems to the court that this charge is so nebulous and indefinite that a jury would have to indulge in speculation in order to arrive at a verdict. . . .

Judge Youngdahl quoted in this connection a part of Justice Jackson's dissenting opinion in the Douds case:

"Attempts of the courts to fathom modern political meditations of an accused would be as futile and mischievous as the efforts in the infamous heresy trials of old to fathom religious beliefs. . . . It is true that in England of olden times men were tried for treason for mental indiscretions such as imagining the death of the king. But our Constitution was intended to end such prosecutions. Only in the darkest periods of human history has any Western government concerned itself with mere belief, however eccentric or mischievous, when it has not matured into overt action; and if that practice survives anywhere, it is in the Communist countries whose philosophies we loathe." [13]

The Lattimore case represents an extraordinarily vindictive attempt by a congressional committee to use the investigating power as a means of punishing an individual whose ideas it deemed offensive. This was not inquiry; it was inquisition. It was not legislative investigation; it was legislative trial. It was not only a legislative invasion of the judicial jurisdiction; it was a subversion of the courts for an unconstitutional congressional purpose. The Senate of the United States is not likely in calmer times to view with pride this conduct on the part of a committee entrusted with its investigating power.[14]

[13] *American Communications Ass'n v. Douds,* 339 U.S. 382, 437 (1950).

[14] In July 1954 the Court of Appeals sustained, eight to one, Judge Youngdahl's dismissal of the key first count in the Lattimore indictment. "The word 'sympathizer,'" the Court of Appeals ruled, "is not of sufficiently certain meaning to sustain a charge of perjury." In addition, the appellate body endorsed Judge Youngdahl's dismissal of count seven, but reversed his dismissal of two other minor counts, three and four.

At this point Leo A. Rover, the United States Attorney in charge of the case, instead of dropping the indictment or appealing to the Supreme Court for restoration of the key count, went before another grand jury and obtained a new indictment, omitting the word "sympathizer" but otherwise merely rephrasing the old first count. The new indictment also presented an even vaguer charge—that Lattimore had lied in asserting that he had never followed the Communist line. Moreover, the prosecutor accused Judge Youngdahl of bias on account of his opinion dismissing the original indictment and sought to have him disqualify himself from trying the case. The judge rejected this attack as "scandalous." Subsequently, he dismissed the new charges, asserting that "to require defendant to go to trial for perjury under charges so formless and obscure would be unprecedented and would make a sham of the Sixth Amendment."

CHAPTER VI

SELF-INCRIMINATION

A man may be punished, even put to death, by the state; but if he is an American or an Englishman or a free man anywhere, he should not be made to prostrate himself before its majesty. *Mea culpa* belongs to a man and his God. It is a plea that cannot be exacted from free men by human authority. To require it is to insist that the state is the superior of the individuals who compose it, instead of their instrument.[1]

I

THE CATCH PHRASE "Fifth Amendment Communist," employed of late so commonly and so carelessly, not only slurs individuals indiscriminately; it also stultifies one of the great safeguards of the Bill of Rights. It reflects condemnation without judgment. The Fourth, Fifth, and Sixth Amendments to the Constitution are concerned with the protection of individuals against the exercise of arbitrary authority by the state; their whole thrust is to place restraints upon law enforcement in order to keep it from becoming despotic. These restraints, essentially procedural in nature, are the essence of a government of laws. As Justice Frankfurter once observed, "The history of liberty has largely been the history of procedural safeguards."[2]

[1] Address by Abe Fortas before the Cleveland Bar Association, March 11, 1954.
[2] *McNabb v. U.S.*, 318 U.S. 332, 347 (1943).

The whole of the Fifth Amendment—the Fifth Article of the Bill of Rights—has always seemed to zealots a mischievous impediment. It confers rights upon men whom they regard as having no claim to society's protection. It places a limitation upon their own power of punishment. Consider what the Fifth Amendment provides:

No person shall be held to answer for a capital, or otherwise infamous crime, unless on a presentment or indictment of a grand jury, except in cases arising in the land or naval forces, or in the militia, when in actual service in time of war or public danger; nor shall any person be subject for the same offense to be twice put in jeopardy of life or limb; nor shall be compelled in any criminal case to be a witness against himself, nor be deprived of life, liberty, or property, without due process of law; nor shall private property be taken for public use, without just compensation.

The clause which has become most controversial in recent years is, of course, the stipulation that no person "shall be compelled in any criminal case to be a witness against himself." The courts long ago asserted that this must be given a broad construction, insuring a witness, in any federal investigation, against being compelled to give testimony that might tend to incriminate him. It allows a witness to refuse to give any information about himself that might prove a link in a chain of evidence leading to his conviction for a crime.

By the time the Constitution of the United States was drafted, the privilege against self-incrimination was a fixture of English Common Law. It had grown in large part out of revulsion against practices of the Court of Star Chamber and the Court of High Commission in the sixteenth and early seventeenth centuries. These tribunals had haled heretics and schismatics before them, interrogating them at random without any sort of indictment or anything in the nature of what today would be considered probable cause. They had explored men's opinions in search of unorthodoxy, commonly employing force and torture to wrest confessions from witnesses. By the latter half of the seventeenth century, the doctrine that a man should not be required to convict himself out of his own mouth had become established beyond question in England and had been adopted as a tenet of the law in some of the American colonies. It was included in the Virginia Bill of Rights in 1776 and was thereafter made part of the constitutions of six or seven of the original states. Ultimately all but two of the states of the Union included it in their constitutions.

But beyond the protest against random questioning and torture, the privilege against self-incrimination was rooted in respect for the human personality and in a feeling that no one should be compelled to bring about his own undoing. The privilege stands, indeed, as one of the symbols of man's striving for individual dignity. It marks one of the great limitations upon governmental power. Dean Erwin N. Griswold of the Harvard Law School has said that "the privilege against self-incrimination is one of the great landmarks in man's struggle to make himself civilized." [3]

In recent years the privilege against self-incrimination has fallen into a measure of disrepute. It has been, on the one hand, rather frequently abused by witnesses who employed it as a device to avoid incriminating friends and associates or as a means of protesting against congressional inquiries of which they disapproved. On the other hand, it has been transformed by overzealous congressional investigators from a safeguard into a snare. So many extralegal penalties are attached to pleading it that today a witness can avail himself of the constitutional immunity against self-incrimination only at considerable risk and sacrifice.

The reason is that pleading this privilege is generally taken to be conclusive acknowledgment of guilt. Senator McCarthy in particular has fostered the fallacy that the protection of the Fifth Amendment can be properly claimed only by those who would be certain to suffer conviction of a crime as a result of answering his questions truthfully. He has made the privilege seem, in short, solely a protection for the guilty.

Unfortunately this fallacy has received support from more im-

[3] Address to the Massachusetts Bar Association, Springfield, Massachusetts, February 5, 1954.

pressive and more respectable sources as well. It is an easy assumption for the unsophisticated or the unscrupulous. But it is surprising to find it taken for granted by a commission of jurists—a former Attorney General of the United States among them—who advised the Secretary General of the United Nations in December 1952 on the policy he ought to follow respecting United Nations employees who pleaded the Fifth Amendment when summoned before the Senate Internal Security Subcommittee and questioned about present or past membership in the Communist party.

"If in reliance upon this privilege a person refuses to answer a question," the commission reported, "he is only justified in doing so if he believes or is advised that in answering he would become a witness against himself." This places a witness, according to the commission, in a "dilemma"—"the dilemma that either his answer would have been self-incriminatory or if not he has invoked his constitutional privilege without just cause. . . . Either his answers would have incriminated him or he had no right to claim privilege. In neither case, in our opinion, can he be heard to say that his resort to privilege was unnecessary or unjustified."

This is technically accurate if it is read to mean that a witness may properly plead the privilege only if his answer would place him in some jeopardy; but it seems to assume that the privilege against self-incrimination was intended only as a protection for the guilty. It was intended, of course, primarily as a protection for the innocent. The fact that guilty persons may seek its sanctuary, just as they may take refuge in the constitutional prohibition against unreasonable searches and seizures, indicates no more than that the founders of the Republic recognized that it was better to run the risk of letting some guilty persons escape punishment than to permit persecution of the innocent. Such restraints upon governmental authority were part of the price the founders deemed it prudent to pay for the sake of maintaining a free society.

It runs counter to common sense to suppose that those who

included the privilege against self-incrimination in the Fifth Amendment did so primarily for the purpose of protecting the guilty—or, as Senator McCarthy would no doubt put it, for the sake of coddling Communists. The founders were idealists but neither sentimentalists nor fools.

A refusal to answer questions is not necessarily an acknowledgment of guilt. A person may reasonably and properly decline to make admissions which, in the circumstances of a particular situation, could be considered evidence of complicity in a crime of which he is actually innocent. Suppose, for instance, he were innocently present at the scene of a crime and knew himself to be suspected, or even accused by others, of having committed it; suppose he had killed another man in self-defense or by accident, innocently but under conditions which would subject him to suspicion of evil intent. To make any admissions in such circumstances would be to put himself in jeopardy. It would in effect, as Dean Griswold has pointed out, shift the burden of proof to him so that he would have to prove his own innocence.[4]

There can scarcely be any question as to the right of an American to invoke the Fifth Amendment in situations such as these. Sometimes, however—and no doubt frequently in recent years— the Fifth Amendment is invoked less validly in situations it was not intended to cover, although the persons who invoke it may be innocent of the offense imputed to them. It is used on occasion by persons convinced that the whole direction and purpose of a congressional inquiry are evil and dangerous as a method of expressing protest. It is, as it were, a form of passive resistance to methods that seem abhorrent. It serves as a technique of revolt against what is considered a species of governmental despotism.

Persons who use the Fifth Amendment in this way have no legal right to do so. Perhaps, however, there is an element of moral right —or at least of poetic justice—in their resort to it. It amounts to an invalid defense against an unjustifiable inquisitorial attack. It operates to fulfill what Abe Fortas has called the fundamental function of the privilege against self-incrimination—that is, to

4 Ibid.

bring about "a basic adjustment of the power and rights of the individual, and of the state." [5]

The fact remains that, however mistaken such pleaders of the Fifth Amendment may be, they are not necessarily guilty persons. They may be entirely innocent, though misguided, protestants. Innocent persons sometimes plead the Fifth Amendment as a means of avoiding the perils of a perjury prosecution. And their innocence is in no way diminished by the dubious legality of this recourse. The experience of Owen Lattimore, indicted for perjury after categorically denying any Communist sympathies, stands as a strong spur to this kind of self-protection.

Any witness before a congressional investigating committee who denies Communist affiliations or sympathies runs a real risk of having to defend himself against a perjury charge, and the defense may be exceedingly difficult. Some of the investigating committees turn readily, and with unreserved credulity, to one or another of an always available stable of ex-Communist professional witnesses, prepared at a moment's notice to remember anything about anybody at any time, no matter how remote in the past. Some of these witnesses possess reservoirs of recollection which, like the miraculous pitcher of Baucis and Philemon, seem to replenish themselves whenever a congressional interrogator finds himself thirsty for new headlines.

It is, besides, a curiosity of recent congressional investigations that the ex-Communists seem always to make their accusations with impunity, while those who dare to contradict them are called upon to vindicate themselves. Such contradiction is especially hazardous in the case of persons who may have had left-wing associations or expressed left-wing opinions without ever having been members of the Communist party. If a man long ago joined organizations which subsequently came to be called Communist fronts, if he voiced criticism of the FBI or the House Committee on Un-American Activities, if he favored racial equality or questioned the ability of Chiang Kai-shek to invade and conquer the mainland of China, it is not altogether beyond comprehension,

[5] Fortas, op. cit.

however foolish it may seem, that he should hesitate to deny under oath the accusation of an ex-Communist that he was once a party member or a party sympathizer. If the denial should result in a perjury indictment, the scales of justice, given the present slant of public opinion, might seem heavily weighted against him. Sometimes, in such a situation, innocent men choose the privilege against self-incrimination in order to escape the expense and hazard and notoriety of a perjury trial.

This is not to say that innocent men are legally entitled to claim the privilege as an escape from telling the truth because of such fears. The consensus among lawyers appears to be that such claiming of the privilege is not warranted. The privilege can be properly claimed only as a protection against compulsory disclosure of past conduct which may be used as evidence in a criminal prosecution. Nevertheless, unwarranted claims of this sort are commonly upheld because of the manifest difficulty of determining when and whether an answer to a question might, in fact, prove "incriminating." Consequently, when accused individuals see committees trying to trap them and threatening them with prosecution for perjury, they are often tempted to seek shelter under the Fifth Amendment. It would be unintelligent as well as unjust to take it for granted that all such claimants of the privilege have guilty knowledge to conceal.

A number of persons have availed themselves of the Fifth Amendment in order to avoid being forced to act as informers. The privilege was certainly not intended to permit witnesses to avoid a citizen's ordinary obligation to aid in the administration of justice. No one, save a doctor, lawyer, or priest in connection with professional confidences, or a wife or husband in connection with the confidences of a spouse, may lawfully refuse to tell a court or a committee what he knows about the activities of others when that knowledge is pertinent to a legitimate inquiry—unless these activities, or his knowledge of them, might be a link in a chain of evidence that could lead to his own conviction. The privilege is strictly a personal one. Nevertheless, men of conscience and decency are understandably reluctant to tell about past political indiscretions of friends or former associates—especially if they feel that the indiscretions were entirely innocent and entirely in the past. This is, perhaps, the most common reason for recourse to the Fifth Amendment. The privilege is often pleaded by persons who would be willing enough to waive it and to talk about themselves, but who fear that the waiver might result in their being forced to turn informer.

A candid and illuminating instance of this kind was provided by the distinguished playwright Lillian Hellman when she was summoned before the House Committee on Un-American Activities in May 1952. She wrote to the committee chairman just prior to her public appearance:

I am not willing, now or in the future, to bring bad trouble to people who, in my past association with them, were completely innocent of any talk or any action that was disloyal or subversive. I do not like subversion or disloyalty in any form, and if I had ever seen any I would have considered it my duty to have reported it to the proper authorities. But to hurt innocent people whom I knew many years ago in order to save myself is, to me, inhuman and indecent and dishonorable. . . .

I am prepared to waive the privilege against self-incrimination and to tell you anything you wish to know about my views or actions, if your committee will agree to refrain from asking me to name other people. If the committee is unwilling to give me this assurance, I will be forced to plead the privilege of the Fifth Amendment at the hearing.

The committee chairman declined to give Miss Hellman the assurance she sought. She therefore availed herself of the privilege against self-incrimination, to which she was indubitably entitled, and refused to testify at all. The reason for Miss Hellman's resort to the privilege lay, plainly, not in any guilty desire to conceal information about herself; it lay, rather, in the strange doctrine of waiver set forth by the Supreme Court in the Rogers case in 1951.[6] A year earlier, in the Blau case, the court had ruled that questions as to connections with the Communist party are subject to the privilege against self-incrimination since they call for disclosure of facts tending to incriminate under the Smith Act—the act

[6] *Rogers* v. *U.S.*, 340 U.S. 367 (1951).

under which Communist party leaders were convicted and sentenced to prison.[7]

Jane Rogers was summoned before a federal grand jury and, without claiming any privilege under the Fifth Amendment, testified candidly that she had been the treasurer of the Communist party of Denver and, upon completion of her term of office, had turned the books and records of the party over to her successor. She was thereupon asked to name her successor but declined to do so, simply asserting that "I don't feel that I should subject a person or persons to the same thing that I'm going through."

Mrs. Rogers was taken before a federal district judge and, while awaiting her turn to be heard by him, listened to an oral argument in which another alleged party member pleaded the privilege against self-incrimination and was excused from answering questions. This was apparently an eye-opener to her. She was asked by the judge if she still persisted in refusing to answer the questions put to her in the grand-jury room. On the basis of her brief law course of the morning, she said, "Well, as I said before, I'm a very honest person and I'm not acquainted with the tricks of legal procedure, but I understand from the reading of these cases this morning that I am—and I do have a right to refuse to answer these questions, on the basis that they would tend to incriminate me, and you read it yourself, that I have a right to decide that."

Her legal learning was inadequate, however. The judge declared that she had no right to refuse to testify and imposed a sentence of four months for contempt. The Tenth Circuit Court of Appeals upheld his view, and so, ultimately, did the Supreme Court, although with a most vigorous dissenting opinion by Justice Black, in which Justices Frankfurter and Douglas joined.

Chief Justice Vinson, speaking for the majority of the Supreme Court, declared that the original refusal to answer was unwarranted, "since a refusal to answer cannot be justified by a desire to protect others from punishment, much less to protect another from interrogation by a grand jury." Moreover, the Chief Justice went on, Mrs. Rogers had already "waived her privilege of silence

[7] *Blau* v. *U.S.*, 340 U.S. 159 (1950).

when she freely answered criminating questions relating to her connection with the Communist party." Identifying the person or persons to whom she turned over the party records, he reasoned, would be a mere detail which she was not privileged to withhold since it could not materially increase the danger of prosecution.

"Today's holding," said Justice Black prophetically, "creates this dilemma for witnesses: on the one hand, they risk imprisonment for contempt by asserting the privilege prematurely; on the other, they might lose the privilege if they answer a single question. The court's view makes the protection depend on timing so refined that lawyers, let alone laymen, will have difficulty in knowing when to claim it." In addition, the dissenting Justice pointed out, Mrs. Rogers' answer "would not only have been relevant in any future prosecution of petitioner for violation of the Smith Act, but also her conviction might depend on testimony of the witnesses she was thus asked to identify. For these reasons the question sought a disclosure which would have been incriminating to the highest degree."

Justice Black's warning about the mischievous propensities of the court's waiver doctrine has been abundantly borne out by subsequent experience. Lawyers, fearful that their clients might waive the privilege by answering a question, have advised them to plead the Fifth Amendment in response to all questions, and a steady stream of witnesses has taken refuge in the privilege long before there was need to do so and even when doing so could not fail to prove humiliating and painful.

It has become a favorite trick of some congressional investigators to ask such witnesses questions to which the interrogators know well that a truthful answer would be entirely creditable but which they also know the witness feels obliged to leave unanswered in order to preserve his privilege. This is, at least in large part, the explanation for the frequent refusal of witnesses to deny the most horrendous offenses, such as espionage. They believe that they dare not answer even this question if they are to avoid a waiver of their right to refuse other answers.

The plain fact of the matter is that these investigators are delighted when witnesses plead the Fifth Amendment. Proof of this is to be found in the rarity with which they challenge the plea, even when resort to it is obviously invalid. Nothing serves their purpose better than a pleading of the privilege. And the more outlandish the occasion, the better they like it. They are quick enough to threaten any witness with contempt proceedings if he refuses to answer on grounds of the First Amendment or on grounds of a general unwillingness to cooperate with the committee. But they accept recourse to the Fifth Amendment because they take it—and have now taught a large part of the American public to take it—as an outright admission of complicity in the Communist conspiracy.

They are little concerned with shadings or degrees of complicity. They are quite content, as a rule, to let the matter go with a broad undefined implication that the silent witness—who may have been guilty of nothing more than a youthful flirtation with the Communist party—is a blackhearted and dangerous traitor to the United States. And they frequently seem not nearly so much interested in any information the witness might be able to furnish to the committee as in the witness's humiliation and self-destruction. An indication of this is to be found in the common practice of examining witnesses first in executive session and, if they plead the privilege there, of summoning them to do the same thing all over again in a public hearing.

Nothing more clearly illustrates the extent to which the congressional investigating committee has become a contemporary reproduction of the seventeenth-century Court of Star Chamber than this system of screening and selecting witnesses for public display. It regularly summons men and women before it in closed proceedings on mere suspicion or irresponsible accusation; if they show themselves willing and able to deny present or past membership in the Communist party, it commonly has no further use for them. But if they acknowledge present or past membership in the Communist party, or, better still from the committee's point of view, refuse to answer questions along this line on the ground that to do so might incriminate them, the committee saves them for a public spectacle. The result is a strengthening of the impression the investigators try to create—that they are infallible in recognizing Communists and uniquely resourceful in exposing them.

Whatever else may be said of this practice, the truth is that it effectively turns the tables on those who would use the Fifth Amendment as a form of protest against investigating methods. They merely play into the committee's hands. Far from creating a public impression that the investigators are ruthless inquisitors careless of the civil rights of those summoned before them, they manage instead to create an impression that Communists abound in the areas being investigated. The pleaders of the Fifth Amendment, permitted to enjoy its refuge without challenge from the investigators, emerge without any of the glamour of martyrdom. They seem merely frightened creatures running shamefacedly for cover because they are incapable of defending themselves.

The result could not be otherwise. The American public is unlikely to spring to the defense of individuals unwilling to speak up in their own defense. Their protest is made ambiguously and timorously. The privilege against self-incrimination was never meant to be an instrument of social protest. As Professor Bernard Meltzer of the University of Chicago Law School observed in a distinguished essay on the uses of the Fifth Amendment, "The privilege does not, in short, make honest or effective protest possible at bargain prices." [8]

Among persons who consider congressional inquiry into political opinion odious, there is a widespread feeling that pleaders of the Fifth Amendment ought not to suffer any loss of popular esteem as a result of invoking a constitutional right. They argue that because an inference of guilt is not warranted in law, it ought to be forbidden in public opinion. And they point to the court practice in most states of forbidding a prosecutor to comment on or call attention to the failure of a defendant to take the witness stand in his own defense.

No doubt congressional investigators ought not to invite the

[8] *Bulletin of the Atomic Scientists*, Vol. IX, No. 5 (June 1953), p. 180.

public to draw damaging inferences from a witness's resort to the privilege against self-incrimination. It is a shabby practice. In his article on the Fifth Amendment, Professor Harry Kalven, Jr., a colleague of Mr. Meltzer, observed cogently: "If the public is persuaded that virtually only the guilty will claim the privilege and if each person who does claim it is treated as guilty, in time it will be true that only the guilty can afford to claim it." [9]

This is true, and it is tragic; but it is hard to see how it can be remedied. Congressional investigators are not subject to the discipline imposed upon officers of a court; they are laws unto themselves—which is, indeed, the compelling reason that they should not attempt to do the work of courts. Besides, no matter what restraints investigators might impose upon themselves, the public cannot help drawing invidious inferences from the refusal of a witness to answer questions in a public hearing. To ask the public to disregard the fact that a witness has declined to answer questions on the plea that he might tend to incriminate himself is asking the public to abandon common sense. There is at least an inescapable suspicion in such cases; it is futile to attempt to dispel it, and perhaps the most that can be done is to remind people that in some instances the suspicion may be unjustified.

It must be remembered, moreover, that the Fifth Amendment was intended to save people from being convicted and punished by the state as a consequence of their own admissions; it was not intended to save them from the penalties of unpopularity. The distinction is an important one, and it applies with equal force to the constitutional guarantee of free speech. The First Amendment was meant to keep the state from silencing its citizens; it gives them a right to express opinions their fellow-citizens may abhor, but it does not, and cannot, forbid abhorrence on the part of those fellow-citizens.

When a metropolitan police chief appearing before the Senate Crime Investigating Committee pleaded the Fifth Amendment in response to queries about the sources of his puzzlingly large bank accounts, it was hardly surprising that the community became ex-

[9] Ibid., p. 200.

ceedingly distrustful of him. The Fifth Amendment saved him from making admissions that might have led to his serving a term in prison for accepting bribes from gamblers; it could not reasonably have been expected to save him from losing his job as chief of police. The inference drawn by the public in this situation was inescapable. And surely an insistence upon candor in a police chief—at least in regard to his finances—is not unwarranted.

A distinction may usefully be observed, however, between candor in matters of this sort and candor about political beliefs and associations. It was precisely in order to prevent a random hunting for heterodoxy that the privilege against self-incrimination became established in English law. To make disgrace and dismissal automatic consequences of pleading the privilege in regard to political activity is to drain a constitutional right of much of its meaning.

More and more, recourse to the Fifth Amendment, especially in connection with questions about present or past membership in the Communist party, is coming to be a barrier to the practice of professions, and, indeed, to almost any honorable means of gaining a livelihood. The head of the American Bar Association, William J. Jameson, declared, for example, that all citizens have the right to rely on the privilege of the Fifth Amendment, but that any who do so should be disqualified from law practice, teaching, or government positions of trust.[10] And, according to a United Press story under an Albany, N.Y., dateline of July 16, 1953, "The Albany *Knickerbocker News* announced it had fired Janet Scott because of 'gross misconduct.' Miss Scott, an employee for twenty-five years, refused to answer subcommittee questions [a House Un-American Activities subcommittee] as to whether she is or ever had been a Communist." [11]

At the very least, it would seem that such cases ought to be examined and judged on their individual merits. The traditional American respect for the right of silence in regard to political beliefs, together with the lively possibility that the pleader of the

[10] *Washington Post*, February 11, 1954.
[11] *Washington Post*, July 17, 1953.

privilege is innocent of all wrongdoing, should preclude indiscriminate condemnation and punishment. It serves but a dubious purpose to protect a witness from the perils of prosecution if the price of that protection is to make him an unemployable outcast.

II

When all this has been said, it must be acknowledged, nevertheless, that pleading the privilege against self-incrimination is never likely to seem admirable. It does nothing either to enhance the reputation of the individual pleader or to defend civil liberties for the community as a whole. There are other courses open to individuals questioned about present or past membership in the Communist party—courses that may be difficult and, in some cases, dangerous, but that will nevertheless command more respect than taking refuge in the Fifth Amendment.

The most obvious course is that of candor. This is relatively easy and natural for persons who can say truthfully that they are not and never have been members of the Communist party. As for the danger of a prosecution for perjury growing out of such testimony, it is a danger which it is better to face resolutely than to evade. To assert that hysteria is now so widespread that an innocent man cannot hope to secure vindication in the courts against the accusations of ex-Communist informers is to aggravate the hysteria by behaving hysterically. The truth is still a potent protector in the United States.

For persons who once belonged to the Communist party the course of candor may be a painful one, but it is surely better, and more respectable, to acknowledge the truth than to attempt vainly to conceal it. As a practical matter, a person is certainly no worse off in terms of public opinion, for the public would probably presume him guilty of the worst of the offenses he refused to deny. On the other hand, there would be at least greater respect for a man who said candidly that in his youth he had joined the Communist party, mistakenly believing it to be committed to progressive causes he favored, and that on discovering the party's true nature he had withdrawn from it, rejecting its discipline and its real purposes. There would be nothing in this that a man need be ashamed of. Many good Americans have committed the same error, and for wholly creditable reasons.

But, of course, if a man admits past membership in the party he runs the risk of being asked to give the names of other party members whom he knew. And he has waived his right to refuse under the Fifth Amendment by having talked freely about himself. He then has to choose between turning informer and placing himself in contempt of the committee. A number of witnesses, finding themselves in this situation, have made the latter choice. They have said simply, on grounds of conscience, that they could not or would not name former associates whom they believed innocent of any wrongdoing. This is a position that, however dubious in law, has much moral justification.

An example of this position was afforded by a Philadelphia high-school teacher, Dr. Wilbur Lee Mahaney, Jr., who told a House Un-American Activities subcommittee that he had been a member of the Communist party from about 1935 to 1947 because he mistakenly believed it was devoted to promoting world peace and disarmament. He never engaged in any kind of subversive activity, he said, and never knew anyone who advocated overthrow of the government by force. He then declined, without invoking any kind of constitutional protection—and despite warnings from the committee that he was placing himself in contempt of Congress—to give the names of any of the persons he had known during the period of his membership.

Pressed by subcommittee members to identify former fellow-Communists, Dr. Mahaney replied that "to be an informer . . . is contrary to every tenet of American thinking. . . . It is a matter of deep and abiding conscience with me," he said, and added, "I can only say in accordance with Martin Luther, 'So help me God, I can do no other.' " [12]

A little more than a year later, in May 1954, the Un-American Activities Committee recommended, and the House of Represent-

[12] *Washington Post*, February 17, 1953.

atives approved, a contempt citation of Dr. Mahaney. The Philadelphia School Board suspended him from his job. Under these pressures he came before the committee in July and sought to purge himself. He gave the names of sixteen persons who, he said, were members of the Communist party during the decade of his own membership. Among those he named was a woman who had told the committee she never belonged to the party. And he also identified his former wife as a companion at Communist meetings in late 1944 and early 1945, although she had previously testified that she had attended only one Communist Political Association meeting, and she had refused to name any associates.

One cannot help wondering what exultation the members of the committee felt at having used the majestic power of Congress to achieve this victory over a man's conscience. What manner of investigation is it that will stretch a human spirit upon a rack as cruel in its way as any in the torture chambers of the medieval Inquisition in order to wrest from him, not a confession of his own heresy—he had confessed that long since—but an accusation leveled at old friends, leveled even at the woman he had once promised to honor and to cherish?

What service to security did the committee render by compelling this anguished outcry? The women at whom Mahaney's trembling finger pointed were hardly a menace to the state. What reverence did the committee accord to an honored American tradition by forcing this man to turn informer—to do what every American has been taught from childhood to abhor? The view expressed in Ecclesiasticus that "the talebearer shall defile his own soul and be hated by all" has had, at least until now, almost universal acceptance among free men. What kind of Americanism —what kind of America—is this Committee on Un-American Activities striving to propagate? In Fascist Italy, in Nazi Germany, men were exhorted to inform on their neighbors, even on members of their own families. In Communist Russia the same sort of universal surveillance and informing is encouraged in the name of national security. No doubt this fragmentation of society, this glorification of betrayal, is indispensable to the security of tyrants, but it can contribute nothing to the security of free men. The insistence of congressional inquisitors that witnesses become informers, that they betray associates who so far as they know are guilty only of a past political error, seems a form of Communist brainwashing, a sadistic attempt to break men intellectually and spiritually and leave them drained of all self-respect and self-esteem.

The Senate Internal Security Subcommittee (under the chairmanship of Senator Jenner) showed greater queasiness than its House counterpart about compelling witnesses to serve as informers. In its report on "Subversive Influence in the Educational Process," it observed that "in the case of numerous witnesses, the subcommittee recognized the reluctance of many persons to identify their former associates during their own intermediate stage of transition from the Communist side of the political struggle to the side of free men. Therefore, [it] did not press for names except to ask for some sign or some willingness that would indicate genuine conversion." [13] But this forbearance was not always observed in practice.

It is plain enough that anyone who presumes to withhold from a committee of Congress information which it lawfully demands takes upon himself a heavy burden of responsibility. Only the most deeply conscientious conviction can justify such intransigence. But when it is genuine and sincere, it is much more likely to win understanding among Americans generally than a refusal to answer on a plea of self-incrimination.

A witness who feels certain that the persons with whom he was associated in the party were as idealistic and misguided as himself, and were as innocent of espionage or sabotage or any criminal activity, can in good faith refuse to expose them to odium and humiliation. If these persons have left the party and established respectable positions for themselves which would be destroyed by his disclosures, he can understandably be unwilling to offer them and their families up as sacrificial victims.

This kind of defiance of a congressional committee may be

[13] Senate Internal Security Subcommittee Report, July 17, 1953, p. 4.

altogether unwarranted in law; it may also reflect a mistaken esti-
mate of the particular persons it is intended to protect. Nevertheless, it is an open and candid assumption of individual moral
responsibility of a sort that is expected of men and women in a
society where the individual conscience is recognized as the supreme authority. It is a course more likely to produce public respect and self-respect than any pleading of a constitutional immunity. And if it does not save the pleader from prison, it will save
him at least from an enduring sense of shame.

The one remaining course, open alike to persons who never
joined the Communist party and to those who once were members of it, is the course of protest. If a witness believes deeply that
he cannot in good conscience cooperate with a committee which,
in his judgment, is encroaching improperly on individual freedom,
he can refuse, as Professor Albert Einstein has suggested, to answer any of its questions, even those relating exclusively to himself. But he can make the protest meaningful and effective only
if he is prepared to base it forthrightly on principle and take the
consequences. The consequences may very well entail a heavy and
tragic personal sacrifice; but this sacrifice is at least more likely
than any plea of personal privilege to win the plaudits, and the
gratitude, of posterity. Human freedom sometimes owes a great
deal to just such individual obduracy.

III

In the closing hours of its final session the 83rd Congress passed,
along with a number of other extremist measures sponsored in the
name of anti-communism, a law that empowers congressional
committees to compel the testimony of Fifth Amendment pleaders
by granting them immunity from prosecution in federal courts on
the subject of their admissions. The theory of this so-called "immunity-bath" legislation is that immunity will be granted to a witness when it is more important to the public interest to gain information from him than to prosecute him for a crime. The law,
as adopted after considerable wrangling, provides that a commit-

tee, by a vote of two-thirds of its members, may ask a federal court to issue an order guaranteeing a witness against prosecution in return for his forgoing his privilege against self-incrimination. A committee is empowered to do this only in regard to testimony concerning "attempts to interfere with or endanger the national security or defense of the United States by treason, sabotage, espionage, or the overthrow of its government by force or violence. . . ." The committee must give the Attorney General notice of its intention to seek an immunity order; and he may, if he wishes, argue in opposition to its being granted.

This kind of immunity bath is no novelty. Something akin to it was on the statute books from 1857 to 1862, and was then repealed because it led to gross abuses. Persons who had committed crimes rushed to testify before congressional committees in order to obtain immunity from criminal prosecution. The investigating committees became, during the brief period the law was in force, a kind of bargain-basement confessional where easy absolution could be secured. The danger that this will occur again is only partly obviated by the limitations of the new law, by giving the Attorney General an opportunity to protest and by lodging final determination in a judge. The Attorney General is likely to be complaisant about committee requests involving political purposes with which he is sympathetic—witness, for example, the collaboration between Brownell and Senator Jenner in flogging the dead body of Harry Dexter White—and judges are apt to grant committee requests in the absence of executive opposition.

Moreover, this immunity from prosecution is likely to be counterfeit in important respects. Commenting on one of the proposals being considered by Congress, John W. Davis, a noted authority on constitutional law, pointed out that it did not "purport in express terms to grant immunity from prosecution or penalty under state law" and that "there may still be doubt of the power of Congress so to provide." [14] A state prison may seem just as unpleasant as a federal prison to anyone compelled to be a witness against himself.

[14] Letter, John W. Davis to Senator Harley M. Kilgore, May 14, 1953.

There are, besides, a great many unpleasant consequences and disqualifications attached to membership in so-called "subversive organizations." If a man is required to admit that he belongs, or once belonged, to any group the Attorney General or a congressional committee considers un-American, he will probably find himself barred from public employment and he will probably be unable to get a passport or work in any defense plant or obtain a government contract or receive a license to operate a radio station. These are serious deprivations against which the grant of immunity provides no protection at all. And it is beside the point to say that they would no doubt be imposed anyway as a consequence of pleading the privilege; under the new law they would be imposed as the result of a forced confession.

In an illuminating discussion of the Immunity bill, written before its passage, Leonard B. Boudin observed that the fundamental objection to it "is that the details of a crime are relevant not to legislation but to the prosecution of crime. That is exclusively a grand-jury function under our tripartite system of government. The revelation of crime by congressional committees is especially improper because it deprives the accused of important procedural rights inherent in our accusatorial system. The grand jury historically functions in secrecy to afford protection against improper accusations of crime, an objective which is nullified by today's congressional investigations." [15]

A still more fundamental objection was suggested by Dean Griswold of the Harvard Law School:

In most situations, there are other sources from which relevant testimony may be obtained. Even when immunity from prosecution is granted, there is a certain element inconsistent with our traditions in requiring a person to give testimony which reflects against himself. I recognize that there is no violation of the Constitution in doing so, where immunity is granted. Nevertheless, it seems to me to be more in harmony with our basic traditions, and better judgment, not to require any person to be his own accuser.[16]

[15] Leonard B. Boudin, "The Immunity Bill," *Georgetown Law Journal,* Vol. 42, No. 4 (May 1954), p. 506.
[16] Letter, Erwin N. Griswold to Senator Kilgore, May 13, 1953.

But perhaps the most compelling case against the immunity bath lies in a recognition of its real purpose and its real effect, which are to open up again all those cases in which witnesses invoked the Fifth Amendment before investigating committees when asked about past Communist affiliations.

If the investigating committees were genuinely seeking information from these witnesses and if the information were genuinely important to the national security, the turning of these thumbscrews might be warranted. But in most cases the thumbscrews would be turned only to inflict pain and humiliation, not to elicit information. A grant of immunity would seldom produce anything more than a number of pitiful confessions of past Communist-party membership—a fact already known to the committee —and would lead a number of the confessors to debase themselves by naming former associates. "This bill," said Representative Emanuel Celler when the immunity bath was being debated, "will encourage informers, will indemnify rogues." [17] Indeed, it is not too much to say that it will corrupt the consciences of many men and compel them to do what they—and most of their fellow-Americans in their hearts—consider shameful.

The fact is that in many instances investigating committees deliberately allowed witnesses to plead the Fifth Amendment invalidly. As was suggested earlier in this chapter, what the committees often desired to produce was the plea rather than the information. The committees themselves connived in extending the privilege in cases in which they knew very well that the purpose was not to avoid self-incrimination but to avoid being forced to turn informer. What is now proposed, therefore, is that the committees compel testimony in return for granting a meaningless immunity—meaningless because no prosecution was ever really threatened. The only result will be to pillory all over again a great number of helpless, hapless witnesses who have already done penance enough in klieg-lighted congressional hearings. It is not an exhibition worthy of a great republic.

These are political offenders, not criminals. And it was precisely

[17] *Washington Post and Times Herald*, August 28, 1954.

as a protection against persecution for political offenses that the privilege against self-incrimination came into being. The immunity-bath law in this context can serve only to nullify one of the great bulwarks of free men against arbitrary and tyrannical governmental power.

CHAPTER VII

SOCIETY AND THE STATE

The most natural privilege of man, next to the right of acting for himself, is that of combining his exertions with those of his fellow-creatures, and of acting in common with them. I am therefore led to conclude that the right of association is almost as inalienable as the right of personal liberty. No legislator can attack it without impairing the very foundations of society.[1]

I

THE CORNERSTONE of a free society is the concept of limited government. Jefferson's dictum that the least government is the best government propounded a rule that is subject, of course, to flexible interpretation in the light of evolving social needs and circumstances, but one that affords, nevertheless, an illuminating insight into the essential relation between society and the state. The government of a free people is, of necessity, a government of limited jurisdiction. A great many societal interests and activities lie wholly outside the range and grasp of its authority.

This is, indeed, what significantly distinguishes the libertarian philosophy from the totalitarian. Under an authoritarian rule, such as Russia's, all activities come under the supervision of the state. Industry and entertainment, science and culture,

[1] Alexis de Tocqueville, *Democracy in America,* Galaxy Edition (New York: Oxford University Press, 1946), p. 112.

health, education, and welfare—all are rationalized in the service of what is centrally determined to be "the public interest" and all are carried forward under governmental auspices. There is small room for diversity in such a system. Every institution and every activity must be coordinated and brought into conformity with an authoritatively planned program. Whatever does not directly and demonstrably serve the state is considered dangerously hostile to it and must therefore be extinguished. In short, the state and society are regarded as coextensive and identical.

But in the libertarian view the state is no more than an instrumentality of society—an instrumentality devised to perform functions that cannot as effectively be carried on by individual efforts or by the activities of private, voluntary associations formed for the advancement of special aims and interests. The line between the state and society is never finally drawn in such a system. It advances or recedes, often waveringly, like the tideland juncture of sea and shore, in accordance with changing situations and differing views of how best to deal with them. But somewhere a line is always drawn to set a margin for governmental activity.

The founders of the American Republic, said President A. Whitney Griswold of Yale, "recognized clearly that government was but one, nor at that the noblest, of several means to their end. They understood both the necessity and the limitations of law. On the near, the safe, side of the fences they erected against tyranny, they expected more than mere security for the individual, much more than mere freedom. They expected him to develop his innate qualities of morality and intelligence and to convert these into actions. To these ends they looked upon religion and education as means distinct and separate from government yet essential to it in the total process of achieving the good life." [2]

The government of the United States engages today in a great variety of activities never dreamed of in the philosophy of Thomas Jefferson. Much that was once considered appropriate only for

[2] Baccalaureate Address, Yale University, June 7, 1953.

private enterprise is now undertaken as a matter of course by local or national governmental agencies. Experience has pretty well demonstrated that fire-fighting and crime-detection and the carrying of parcels through the post—to choose a few obvious instances—can be done more satisfactorily through public agencies than, as was the early practice, through private ones. To Americans, however—although not to the English or the French— it has seemed preferable to leave the operation of railroads and of radio, telephone, and telegraph facilities in non-governmental hands. The generation of electric power, the building of houses, the non-military development of atomic energy, have been entrusted mainly to competing private enterprisers, with a stimulating admixture of governmental pilot projects and subsidization. Public schools and private schools have been fostered side by side at every level of education. The care of the aged, the indigent, and the ill, once left almost entirely to private philanthropy in this country, has now been shouldered in some measure by public authorities.

The expansion of governmental activity which has taken effect in the United States—and which has gone forward at an accelerating pace during the past quarter of a century—has been, at least until very recently, confined almost entirely to the sphere of economic interests. It has been pragmatically determined in accordance with the prevailing convictions of the society as to its needs. The disappearance of the American frontier, the growth of mammoth industrial enterprises, the irreversible integration of the national economy, have led to a large measure of governmental intervention in private economic affairs.

Untrammeled private enterprise and individual initiative—the dynamic factors in American economic growth—led to dangers of monopoly control or of rule by private interests that threatened the independence and the real liberty of great numbers of Americans. The government has had to enforce responsibility and restraint upon private enterprise in order to preserve the equality of opportunity that had made it dynamic. Of this kind of governmental intervention in economic affairs, it can fairly be said that it fulfilled what John Locke called the true function of law:

> Law, in its true notion, is not so much the limitation as the direction of a free and intelligent agent to his proper interest, and prescribes no farther than is for the general good of those under that law. Could they be happier without it, the law, as a useless thing, would of itself vanish; and that ill deserves the name of confinement which hedges us in only from bogs and precipices. So that, however it may be mistaken, the end of law is not to abolish or restrain, but to preserve and enlarge freedom. For in all the states of created beings capable of laws, where there is no law there is no freedom. For liberty is to be free from restraint and violence from others, which cannot be where there is no law; and is not, as we are told, "a liberty for every man to do what he lists." For who could be free, when every other man's humour might domineer over him? [3]

Nevertheless, the extension of state power must always be a matter of jealous concern to free men. It gives rise to two grave dangers. One is that reliance on the government to perform a great variety of services may, if carried to imprudent extremes, paralyze the free play of individual initiative, which has contributed so much—in the release of human energy, in the encouragement of innovation and experimentation, and in the development of new goods and services—to the well-being of American life. The other danger is that acceptance of ranging governmental activity in economic affairs may make the American people unconsciously hospitable to governmental interference in areas where the state ought never to intrude—the areas of expression, association, and conscience.

Big government is undoubtedly an imperative of modern times. Total government is not. The most ominous aspect of the contemporary use of the congressional investigating power is that it thrusts the state into intellectual and spiritual activities of society which have traditionally been left—and ought to be left—to non-governmental management. This use of the investigating power carries with it inescapable implications of governmental control.

[3] John Locke, *Of Civil Government*, Everyman's Library, pp. 143–44.

"Those who won our independence," said Justice Brandeis in the greatest of his opinions, "believed that the final end of the state was to make men free to develop their faculties." [4] In economic matters, where unqualified freedom for some men may forge fetters for others, this means the imposition of equitable governmental rules. But in matters of the mind and the spirit, individual freedom may be considered an absolute. The free expression of ideas—even of ideas considered odious and dangerous—does nothing to foreclose the expression of competing ideas. And it is the clash of these ideas that is the essence of the democratic process. Diversity of opinion is a distinguishing and indispensable characteristic of a free society. Only where it exists and is afforded uninhibited expression can men be considered genuinely self-governing; only where it exists can the powers of government be said to derive from the genuinely voluntary consent of the governed.

Freedom of expression, as Tocqueville noted in the observation quoted at the head of this chapter, is inseparably linked to freedom of association. Men are likely to make themselves heard most effectively when they speak in unison. In the United States the motive force of political action comes from voluntary associations of like-minded citizens who join hands transiently for the promotion of purposes they have in common. These associations possess much more sense of direction and are much more the real movers of public opinion than the major political parties, which tend to be loose agglomerations of special-interest groups, striving to be all things to all men and interested more in political office than in principles or policies.

The freedom accorded voluntary associations in the United States has, on the whole, worked well for the American people. If it has produced a Babel of voices, some of them advocating foolish or dangerous doctrines, it has also produced counterbalancing common sense. The democratic process is an experimental process—a process in which irresponsibility cannot be outlawed so long as it is confined to expression and in which the sifting

[4] *Whitney* v. *California*, 274 U.S. 357 (1927).

of sense from nonsense must be left to the intelligence of the people.

Reliance on this process was breached by Congress when it passed the Smith Act in 1940, penalizing the advocacy of overthrowing the government by force or violence—as though Americans could not be counted on to reject such advocacy of their own volition. It was breached again by the McCarran Internal Security Act of 1950, which authorized, in effect, a licensing of voluntary associations by imposing special restrictions on those that might be officially declared "Communist-action" or "Communist-front" organizations. It was further breached by the Communist Control Act of 1954, which formally proscribed an association, the Communist party, that had already been rendered innocuous by the techniques of freedom. The Communist party has undoubtedly come more and more to take on the characteristics of a conspiracy; but suppression has aggravated, not diminished, these characteristics. An astute observation made by Tocqueville in 1835 might well be pondered in this connection: "In countries where associations are free, secret societies are unknown. In America there are numerous factions, but no conspiracies." [5]

The limitations imposed by law on unpopular associations in the field of political action have been matched by what may prove to be an even more mischievous incursion into affairs that have traditionally been considered immune from governmental regulation. Congress has launched a series of investigations, with which the remainder of this chapter will be concerned, into the activities of certain tax-exempt foundations, churches, and universities. No doubt Congress has the power to investigate institutions to which it grants tax exemption, if for no other reason than to determine if the grant should be continued. But to acknowledge that this power exists is by no means to say that it ought to be exercised. The use of it carries inescapable implications of control. And, indeed, the manner in which the Reece Committee investigated foundations, the Velde Committee churches, and the

[5] Tocqueville, op. cit., p. 112.

Jenner Subcommittee universities, revealed an unmistakable tendency to bring these institutions under the authority of the state.
These investigations cast a totalitarian shadow.

"In a democracy," said Spinoza long ago, "everyone submits
to the control of authority over his actions but not over his judgment and reason. What shall be accepted as true or rejected as
false, or what opinions should actuate men in their worship of
God, are questions falling within a man's natural right, which he
cannot abdicate even with his own consent."

II

The tax-exempt foundations, particularly those which have ex-
cited congressional curiosity and criticism, are legal devices for
channeling private fortunes into the service of the public interest.
"Since the very beginning of our history," observed H. Rowan
Gaither, Jr., president of the Ford Foundation, "the American
people have recognized a duty to give to their churches and
schools and to charitable causes, and they have looked upon the
right to join together in private action for the public welfare as
an important element in the idea of a free society." [6] The concepts
of public welfare reflected by this sort of private action have been
diverse. They have included, along with direct support of religious, educational, medical, and charitable institutions, encouragement of the arts and literature, the fostering of scientific research, the investigation of social, economic, and political problems, experimentation in new techniques for improving human relations at local, national, and international levels, and countless
other activities which seemed to donors and trustees to hold some
reasonable hope of enabling men to live together more happily.
Operating on a non-profit basis under charters issued to them by
Congress or by state governments, they have been granted exemption from the payment of taxes because of the recognition that
their efforts hold at least a hope for the service of society.

[6] Statement to the Special House of Representatives Committee to Investigate Tax-Exempt Foundations, July 16, 1954.

Tax exemption was granted as an encouragement to the aims of the foundations and on condition that they refrain from political, propagandistic, or profit-making activities. It was not intended to serve as a pretext for making them subject to government supervision. The Internal Revenue Service has a continuing duty, of course, to see to it that the required restraints are observed. But beyond this, the foundations were meant to be, and imperatively need to be, wholly independent of governmental control.

They need independence of the government for two compelling reasons. One is that independence enables them to undertake certain tasks that it would be difficult for the government itself to undertake. Some of their research projects violate taboos or affront popular prejudices; some of their funds may be expended for ventures likely to be characterized as boondoggles; some of their grants are made to individuals or organizations that may be unpopular, and they are made sometimes on an arbitrarily selective basis; some of their undertakings seem so idealistic or offer so remote a hope of success as to make them unsuitable for the investment of tax dollars. No government dependent upon popular support could comfortably take on chores of this sort. The foundations, by reason of their independence and their dedication to certain goals, can assume financial risks that the government, administering public funds, would not, and indeed should not, incur. There are, in point of fact, numerous studies and experiments fostered by the foundations which might well be blighted if they were carried forward under the pressures toward conformity that would be entailed in governmental sponsorship.

The second, and manifestly related, reason that foundations need independence of the government is that many of their projects are, and ought to be, critical of the government and of established political institutions. A free society is always in need of the kind of investigation that questions its own values and prevailing patterns. Foundations are peculiarly able to lend support to this kind of questioning. Thus they serve in a vital way as censors of the government. They are instrumentalities of society as distinct from the state.

It is hardly surprising, therefore, that foundations striving to fulfill this function should encounter hostility from some members of the legislature. The foundations that served society best became natural targets for those who regarded any deviation from orthodoxy as evidence of disloyalty. In the spring of 1952 the late E. E. Cox, an influential member of the House of Representatives from Georgia, obtained authorization and an appropriation of seventy-five thousand dollars to conduct an investigation of tax-exempt foundations "to determine which such foundations and organizations are using their resources for purposes other than the purposes for which they were established, and especially to determine which such foundations and organizations are using their resources for un-American or subversive activities or for purposes not in the interest or tradition of the United States."

"The ultimate effect of this resolution," said Representative Robert Hale of Maine prophetically, "will be to discourage charitable foundations and those who might otherwise contribute to them or endow them. Under it, it would be easy to establish congressional censorship of all teachings and teachers in our colleges and universities, thus putting an end to any semblance of academic freedom."

Congressman Cox had given a pretty good indication of the ax he was going to grind when he told the House of Representatives a year or so before his committee went into operation: "The Rockefeller Foundation, whose funds have been used to finance individuals and organizations whose business it has been to get communism into the private and public schools of the country, to talk down America and to play up Russia, must take its share of the blame for the swing of the professors and students in China to communism during the years preceding the successful Red revolution in China."

The method of investigation pursued by the Cox Committee was to summon before it trustees and administrators of foundations and question them concerning the political beliefs and associations of the individual beneficiaries of their grants. Looking for Communist infiltration, the committee had no difficulty in uncovering what it took to be evidence of what it sought. It found such evidence in the fact that Alger Hiss had at one time been president of the Carnegie Endowment for International Peace, that Frederick Vanderbilt Field had once been secretary of the Institute of Pacific Relations, and that some foundations had made grants to some individuals who had belonged to organizations of which the committee disapproved—generally organizations the House Committee on Un-American Activities had called "Communist fronts."

The committee listened gravely to such witnesses as Louis Budenz, for years an official of the Communist party, who testified that thirty persons who received research grants from tax-exempt foundations or who helped to dispense such grants were either Communist cardholders or under Communist "discipline." The committee allowed Budenz, under the protection of its immunity from suits for slander and without requiring him to furnish any proof whatever of what he said, to name these persons publicly—many of them distinguished and respected teachers who made categorical denials of the allegations.

A few of the foundation officials responded to this method of inquiry with robust indignation. One of the most eminent, Dr. Henry Allen Moe, who for twenty-five years has been the secretary of the John Simon Guggenheim Memorial Foundation, a resourceful discoverer of genius and a beneficent prodder of creative effort, gave the committee some sorely needed perspective on the function of the foundations. Of course, he acknowledged, his foundation had made some grants that later turned out to be "mistakes," but he resolutely refused to condemn as among these "mistakes" such grants as those given to the noted composer Aaron Copland, or to a distinguished Yale Law School professor, Thomas I. Emerson, merely because these men had associated with certain groups that had come under congressional attack.

"There is a correlation," Mr. Moe told the committee, "between academic eminence and political naïveté." This is perhaps no more than to say that men of uncommon intellectual capacity are likely to be nonconformists. And these are precisely the men that any foundation encouraging creative work must seek. "If you pick the gilt-edged," Mr. Moe put it, "you get two per cent; in the particular business I am in you take risks and you play for higher stakes."

Chester Barnard, a former president of the Rockefeller Foundation, expressed much the same thought in different words: "It has not been the practice of the Rockefeller Foundation to inquire into the politics, religion, skin color, or racial origin of applicants for its grants and fellowships. The only personal criteria are two: the applicant's technical competence and his integrity as a scholar." Dr. Robert M. Hutchins, then an official of the Ford Foundation, warned the committee against the dangers of hunting for subversives among educators. "The thing you must do to the uttermost possible limits," he said, "is to guarantee those men the freedom to think and to express themselves."

A number of foundation spokesmen seemed, however, to accept the premises of the committee's investigation with docility and, while defending their own institutions, offered no challenge to the congressional intrusion into their domain. The reward of this complaisance was that when the committee filed its report on January 2, 1953 (Representative Cox having died a few days earlier), the foundations were praised for their cooperation in the inquiry and were exonerated from any "obstruction, delay, or resentment." "On balance," said the committee report, "the record of the foundations is good. . . . The foundation, once considered a boon to society, now seems to be a vital and essential factor in our progress."

One cannot help wondering if the foundations paid too high a price for this praise. The fact that they emerged uncensured affords no assurance that they emerged unscathed. The foundations were given notice by the Cox Committee that if they wanted to remain in the good graces of Congress they had better not give any more fellowships to Aaron Copland, or to any musician, writer, artist, or researcher whose political opinions might be tinged with unorthodoxy; they were given notice that they had better not make any grants to colleges that retain on their faculties teachers named by Louis Budenz.

This may prove very inhibiting to foundations whose business it is to support unorthodoxy. The test of how largely they escaped injury in their ordeal by investigation will be the independence they display in the future.[7] It will be a great loss to society if they are chastened and timorous. Their situation is somewhat reminiscent of the old story about two men who got into an altercation over a dice game. One of them whipped out a razor and made a violent swoosh in the neighborhood of the other's neck. The second watched the first put the razor back in his pocket and jeered, "Yah, you never touched me." To which the first man said, "That's what you think, brother. But just wait until you try to turn your head." The foundations need to be able to turn their heads to the left as well as to the right in the years ahead.

One clear consequence of their docility before the Cox Committee was that two years later they found themselves faced with another investigation, this time under the direction of Representative B. Carroll Reece of Tennessee. Perhaps, like the motion-picture industry, which has made itself, through "cooperation," a perennial target for congressional investigators, the foundations will find that they are considered fair game by any member of Congress desirous of seeing his name in headlines. Like the motion-picture industry, the foundations have given away the moral basis of resistance to congressional investigation. They cannot now easily assert, on grounds of principle, that Congress ought not to exercise authority over their activities.

[7] "Today, timidity characterizes too much of our current corporate and individual giving. Misunderstanding of voluntary associations and their importance to our way of life impairs our progress and restrains worth-while citizen activity in many ways. There is an unfortunate tendency for donors to select the safe and sure—safe in the sense that few will criticize the gift; sure in that the result of the gift may be predicted. This tendency, if it persists, will create a philanthropic imbalance by withholding support from areas which must be developed if we are to advance on a broad front. For progress requires the breaking of new and uncertain ground, and often it is surrounded by debate and controversy. It is the antithesis of the safe and the sure."—The Ford Foundation, Annual Report for 1953, pp. 24–25.

Reece's approach to the foundations was somewhat more doc-
trinaire than Cox's. Asserting that the Cox Committee had done
an incomplete job, Reece broached the need for another study by
a savage attack on the Ford Foundation, the National Education
Association, the Public Affairs Committee, and a number of other
organizations. "More and more," he declared, "the wealth of
America is going into the tax-exempt foundations and relatively
few of them tend to the right." His concern, he said, was "not so
much with subversion as it is the extent to which the money of
tax-exempt foundations is used for propaganda and to influence
public opinion for the support of certain types of ideologies that
tend to the left."

Reece's method was quite different from Cox's. He recruited a
staff that shared his jaundiced view of the foundations and then
let it report his prejudices in public. The opening report, a disser-
tation by the committee's director of research, Norman Dodd, delivered May 16, 1954, blandly announced that "during the four
years, 1933–1936, a change took place which was so drastic as
to constitute a 'revolution,'" that "the responsibility for the economic welfare of the American people had been transferred heavily to the executive branch of the federal government," and that
"a corresponding change in education had taken place from an
impetus outside the local community, and that this 'revolution'
had occurred without violence and with the full consent of an
overwhelming majority of the electorate." The staff studies
showed, said Mr. Dodd, that this "revolution" "could not have occurred peacefully, or with the consent of the majority, unless
education in the United States had prepared in advance to en-
dorse it." [8]

From this modest premise Dodd went on to reveal the discovery
in ensuing staff studies of a "purposeful relationship" between
foundations and the executive branch of the federal government,
aimed, among other things, at

[8] "Report from Norman Dodd, Director of Research, Covering His Direction of the Staff of The Special Committee of The House of Representatives
to Investigate Tax-Exempt Foundations for the Six Months' Period November 1, 1953–April 30, 1954."

Directing education in the United States toward an international viewpoint and discrediting the traditions to which it had been dedicated.

Decreasing the dependency of education upon the resources of the local community and freeing it from many of the natural safeguards inherent in this American tradition.

Changing both school and college curricula to the point where they sometimes denied the principles underlying the American way of life.

Financing experiments designed to determine the most effective means by which education could be pressed into service of a political nature.[9]

Fortunately the committee included one astringent member, Representative Wayne Hays of Ohio, who characterized the thinking that lay behind the staff studies as a "plot psychosis." The committee never got around to hearing more than one or two spokesmen for the foundations, although it allowed others to file written statements rebutting the staff reports. Pendleton Herring, president of the Social Science Research Council, who managed to get his statement read to the committee before public hearings were suspended, had this to say about Dodd's thesis:

In effect, the committee has been presented with an effort to rewrite American history and to explain what has happened in the United States since the turn of the century in terms of a conspiracy. To assert that a revolution has occurred without violence and with the full consent of the electorate, and to imply that peaceful change overwhelmingly supported by the voters of the country is the result of a conspiracy, would strike us as a mere outrageous error if it were not such a fantastic misreading of what we have all witnessed and experienced. To imply that an interlock of individuals unknown to the American public is responsible for basic changes in our national life over the last fifty years, is to belie the responsible statesmanship of the Republic, the lawmaking authority of the Congress, and the good sense of the American people.

By and large, the tax-exempt foundations of the United States, at least the major ones, are managed by responsible citizens quite capable of directing them without congressional supervision. Americans of the highest probity and prestige serve as the trustees

[9] Ibid.

of these foundations. If there is reason to suspect that they have engaged in politics or propaganda or have violated the terms of their charters in any way, the Internal Revenue Service of the Treasury Department has a duty to call them to account; and if there is reason to suspect the Internal Revenue Service of any delinquency in performing this duty, the House Ways and Means Committee has ample authority to study and censure its performance. But to investigate the social philosophy of the foundations and to criticize their individual grants is in a very real sense to displace their trustees, take over their responsibility, and transfer control from private hands to Congress. The effect is to deprive the foundations of their independence.

The encouragement of experimentation, the promotion of diversity, the fostering of orderly social change (even if it is called "social revolution" by congressional investigators), are the proper business of foundations. It is a business which the interference of Congress can only embarrass and impede. In a free-enterprise economy, Congress would surely do well to leave the administration of private funds to private management.

III

"Whatever concerns man and his welfare is a concern of the church and its ministers. Religion has to do with life in its wholeness." This observation is taken from the text of a letter unanimously adopted by the General Council of the Presbyterian Church in the United States of America and issued on November 2, 1953, to members of eight thousand congregations throughout the country. The letter was one of vigorous protest and of stern warning. It contained, among other things, a forthright criticism of the trend taken by some congressional investigations:

Under the plea that the structure of American society is in imminent peril of being shattered by a satanic conspiracy, dangerous developments are taking place today in our national life. Favored by an atmosphere of intense disquiet and suspicion, a subtle but potent assault upon basic human rights is now in progress. Some congressional inquiries have revealed a distinct tendency to become inquisitions. These inquisitions, which find their historic pattern in medieval Spain and in the tribunals of modern totalitarian states, begin to constitute a threat to freedom of thought in this country.

Treason and dissent are being confused. The shrine of conscience and private judgment, which God alone has a right to enter, is being invaded. . . .

While it is not the role of the Christian church to present blueprints for the organization of society and the conduct of government, the church owes it to its own members and to men in general, to draw attention to violations of those spiritual bases of human relationship which have been established by God.

But there are men in political life who would restrict the church to the performance of ritualistic functions. In their own philosophy they appear to have compartmentalized the spirit and believe that it should not intrude in any way in practical affairs. Accordingly, they denounce members of the clergy who presume, as they put it, to "dabble" in politics. Ministers of religion, they assert, should confine themselves to their pulpits—and even there avoid all reference to the contemporary problems of society. Because these men have identified the state with society, they regard all religious concern with social issues as a breaking down of the separation between church and state. Perhaps the best answer to this attitude was given by Dr. A. Powell Davies, the courageous minister of All Souls Unitarian Church in Washington:

How could it make sense that a minister should plead for righteousness in his own parish and keep his silence when righteousness is being mocked in the total sum of all the parishes that constitute a nation? Moreover, no minister is confined within the boundaries of a single parish. He vows to serve the brotherhood of man. Wherever, then, the brotherhood of man requires his service, he must try to serve it.

There are those who say that this may be, but still the duty of a minister is to "stay out of politics" and "preach his sermons from the Bible." Without conceding this, I feel bound to point out that those who demand it have very little knowledge of the Bible. What do they think of the preacher, Nathan, who went to King David and, pointing a finger at him, said, "Thou art the man"? What do they say of Elijah, who publicly condemned Queen Jezebel? Or of Amos, a preacher self-ordained, who went to the capital city of Samaria to tell the nation's rulers that God had grown weary of their sins? Or of Isaiah, a preacher from an aristocratic family who was nevertheless a reformer and who told King Hezekiah that religion had a place in foreign policy? Or of Jeremiah, who foretold the doom of a nation that forsook its moral principles? Or—to come to a conclusive instance—of Jesus, who not only *talked* about cleansing the Temple but who took "a whip of cords" and drove the grafters from its precincts in complete defiance of the alliance of priests and politicians? [10]

It is entirely clear, of course, that ordination does not place any clergyman above the law or give him any immunity from the customary obligations of citizenship. He is as liable to prosecution for crime as any plumber, automobile manufacturer, truck driver, or farmer. He has the same responsibility, and the same right, as any other member of the community to participate in the decisions of the state and to aid in its maintenance of law and order. Thus it is plain enough that Congress has authority to call before one of its committees any minister of religion and require him to give whatever information he has that may be pertinent to the committee's legitimate business.

A House Un-American Activities subcommittee, investigating Communist influence in the Baltimore area in the mid-1930s, called before it on March 18, 1954, the Reverend Dr. John A. Hutchison, a Presbyterian minister and teacher of religion at Williams College. The subcommittee chairman, Representative Donald L. Jackson of California, said by way of preamble that his group had received "sworn testimony to the effect that several ministers were used by the Communist party in Baltimore." The "sworn testimony" came, of course, from professed former Communists. Jackson took pains to declare that the fact that Dr. Hutchison was a minister "should convey no connotation that the committee is investigating religion or any church." He added also that there had been no suggestion or allegation that Dr. Hutchison had ever been a member of the Communist party.

From 1935 to 1937, when he had served as assistant pastor of

[10] A. Powell Davies, *The Urge to Persecute* (Boston: Beacon Press, 1953), pp. vii, viii.

the Brown Memorial Presbyterian Church in Baltimore, Dr. Hutchison admitted, he had been involved in activities of the American League Against War and Fascism. The League, which, for a time, drew into its membership a large number of patriotic Americans concerned about the rise of nazism and fascism and the threat of military aggression from these sources, undoubtedly fell under Communist control. Dr. Hutchison acknowledged that he had been a member of, and had made speeches for, the organization twenty years before, but denied engaging in a protest demonstration when the German cruiser *Emden* visited Baltimore. He also asserted that he had never knowingly done the bidding of Communists in Baltimore and that he had long preached that communism "is an altogether evil thing which free men must resist at all costs." [11] Congressman Jackson asked Dr. Hutchison if the activities of the League Against War and Fascism had been helpful to the Communist party. "Conceivably that is true," Dr. Hutchison replied, adding, however, that "it seems to me the League Against War and Fascism was a washout. It simply didn't succeed at its professed objective. Looking back on it now, I don't think it should have succeeded, and I think it is testimony to the good sense of the American people that it didn't, but it didn't infiltrate what the Communists would call the broad groups of public opinion." [12]

The hearing had a disagreeable consequence for Dr. Hutchison. In the course of his testimony he told the subcommittee that he had never visited the headquarters of the Communist party in Baltimore. This statement was contradicted by three former Communists who appeared as witnesses. Representative Jackson announced that he would refer the conflicting statements to the Department of Justice—a place where anything said by ex-Communist informers seems automatically to be accepted as gospel, while anything said in contradiction, even by a clergyman, is likely to be regarded as the basis for a perjury prosecution.

[11] Hearing before the Committee on Un-American Activities, May 18, 1954, p. 4071.
[12] Ibid., p. 4073.

Granted that Dr. Hutchison's position before the subcommittee was in no way privileged by reason of his being a minister, and granted also that he had the same obligation to testify truthfully as any other citizen, it seems reasonable to raise certain questions about the nature of the committee's investigation. While it cannot be doubted that Congress has power to inquire into the prevalence of Communist influence in Baltimore in the 1930s, perhaps there is room for doubt as to the wisdom and the social utility of such inquiry. It can hardly be said that this dredging up of ancient attitudes sheds much light on contemporary problems.

Similarly, while it cannot be doubted that if Congress has power to question any citizen about his past lawful associations and beliefs it has equal power to question a clergyman in the same way, there is room for doubt as to the propriety of doing so. Dr. Hutchison's conduct clearly violated no law. It may conceivably have raised questions respecting which he was answerable to his parishioners or to the authorities of the Presbyterian Church. But to hold him answerable to a committee of Congress may well have an inhibiting effect on other clergymen; at least it gives them notice that if they enter into associations or engage in activities of which the state disapproves they will be liable to congressional censure. Whatever the power of Congress in this situation, one wonders if it does not, indeed, come perilously close to invading what the General Council of the Presbyterian Church called "the shrine of conscience and private judgment, which God alone has a right to enter."

Despite repeated denials of any intent to investigate "religion or any church," the House Committee on Un-American Activities has shown a remarkable hospitality to former Communists who have delivered sweeping denunciations of the clergy. Perhaps the most egregious case was the publication by the House Committee on Un-American Activities in September 1953 of testimony taken by it in executive session the previous July. The testimony came in part from a man named Joseph Zack Kornfeder, a ubiquitous witness who, by his own account, had joined the Communist party in 1919 and quit it in 1934. He told the committee—which for unexpressed reasons thought the assertion worth putting out under its sponsorship—that six hundred or more American clergymen were "secret" members of the Communist party, and that three or four thousand others were in "the fellow-traveler category." [13]

Witnessing is a highly competitive calling in which the prizes go to the winner of the boldest headlines. Kornfeder was outdone in this inquiry by Benjamin Gitlow, who identified himself as "always one of the top leading officials of the Communist party in the United States from the year 1919 to 1929." Gitlow named names—including some of the most revered names in the ministry. Outstanding among clergymen who, he said, "carried out the instructions of the Communist party or collaborated with it" were Dr. Harry Ward, the Reverend John Haynes Holmes, Rabbi Judah L. Magnes, and Rabbi Stephen S. Wise—distinguished religious leaders who deserved, from a congressional committee, at least a presumption of innocence against the uncorroborated allegations of an ex-Communist. The two rabbis were dead and could not defend themselves.[14] But, for that matter, neither could the Protestants, beyond the issuance of angry, unavailing denials.

Kornfeder and Gitlow were trumped, however, even before their testimony had been made public, by J. B. Matthews, an old and experienced hand at their game. The July 1953 issue of the *American Mercury* contained an article by Matthews entitled "Reds and Our Churches," in which he asserted that the "largest single group supporting the Communist apparatus in the United States today is composed of Protestant clergymen." He went on, moreover, to declare that "some 7000 Protestant clergymen have been drawn during the past 17 years into the network of the Kremlin's conspiracy."

Matthews had just been appointed staff director of Senator Joseph R. McCarthy's investigating subcommittee, and the article, understandably enough, caused a furor. He complained with

[13] Story by William F. Arbogast, Associated Press reporter, *Washington Post*, September 12, 1953.

[14] Dr. Magnes had emigrated to Palestine in 1922, settling permanently in that country. Obviously, therefore, Gitlow must have been referring to events which occurred more than thirty years before he testified.

considerable bitterness that only the first sentence of his article had been quoted by most newspapers, with scant attention given to a subsequent sentence, which acknowledged that "it hardly needs to be said that the vast majority of American Protestant clergymen are loyal to the free institutions of this country. . . ." But the prevailing view of it as an attack on the clergy was not unwarranted. The three Democratic members of the McCarthy Subcommittee, joined by Senator Charles E. Potter of Michigan, a Republican, promptly protested, demanding that Matthews be replaced as head of the subcommittee staff. Senator McCarthy declined to let Matthews go, refusing even at a closed-door subcommittee session to recognize anyone who might make a dismissal motion. A subcommittee chairman, he insisted, can hire and fire whom he pleases without consideration of the views of his colleagues.

McCarthy retreated from this position a few days later after President Eisenhower denounced those who attack "a vast portion" of the clergy—and after resentment had become a tidal wave. He accepted Matthews' resignation with "deep regret." His Republican colleagues, in a "face-saving" gesture, then voted, over Democratic opposition, to give the chairman plenary power in the selection of staff members, and the Democrats forthwith resigned in a body. Six months elapsed before they returned.

The Matthews incident was followed in the same month, July 1953, by a development that dramatized with still greater clarity the implications inherent in congressional questioning of clergymen. A bishop of the Methodist Church, Dr. G. Bromley Oxnam, an outspoken champion of humanitarian and libertarian ideas, who had been made the target of a variety of unsubstantiated slurs under the auspices of the Committee on Un-American Activities, came before that committee at his own request in an effort to correct and clear its "file" concerning him. Not even the stable of reckless professional witnesses subsidized by the committee had had the temerity to call Bishop Oxnam a Communist, but a number of them had referred to him as a dupe or fellow-traveler engaged in activities in and on behalf of Communist-front organizations. For several years official releases issued by the committee had contained false accusations concerning him.

Bishop Oxnam had made repeated attempts, by letters, to refute these allegations and to have the committee's "files" set right about his record. The attempts were of no avail. When Congressman Harold H. Velde of Illinois, chairman of the Committee on Un-American Activities, indicated early in 1953 that his group might investigate alleged subversion among America's churches and churchmen, Bishop Oxnam was one of the first to denounce the idea. His denunciation brought forth a savage attack by a member of the committee, Representative Jackson, on the floor of the House—under the protection, it goes without saying, of congressional immunity. "Bishop Oxnam," said Jackson, "has been to the Communist front what Man-o'-War was to thoroughbred horse-racing, and no one except the good Bishop pays much attention to his fulminations these days. Having served God on Sunday and the Communist front for the balance of the week over such a long period of time, it is no great wonder that the Bishop sees an investigating committee in every vestry." Perhaps it was this that goaded Bishop Oxnam to send the following telegram to the chairman of the committee on June 5, 1953:

Respectfully request opportunity to be heard by your committee to answer false allegations regarding me appearing in your files and released by your committee. Please advise when I may be heard.

An opportunity to be heard was accorded him on July 21, 1953. It included an opportunity to be heard not by the committee alone but by a large audience in the House Caucus Room, and by a still larger audience at radio and television receivers all over the country. The hearing, one of the most dramatic ever staged in that remarkable theater, lasted from two o'clock in the afternoon of Tuesday, July 21, to twelve-twenty in the morning of Wednesday, July 22. Within this span, Bishop Oxnam was allowed fifteen minutes to present a prepared statement. His own impressions can serve best, perhaps, to convey something of the atmosphere and conditions of the hearing room—at least as they affected the protagonist:

> The physical setup a witness faces is most disconcerting. . . . I had insisted upon a public hearing, because I was fearful that unless the press could be present, a committee that had misrepresented an individual over a period of seven years might continue to do so, and the truth of the hearings might never reach the public. I never realized what it would mean to sit before bright lights all afternoon, all through the evening, and into the next morning. . . .
>
> There were, I think, seven microphones or recording devices in front of me, so placed that it was impossible to have my papers before me in any way that gave easy access to the documents. . . . The bright lights necessary for television were directly behind the committee, and therefore were shining in my eyes all the time they were on, throughout the day. It meant that when I lifted my eyes to look toward committee members, I was almost blinded. It was extremely difficult to read from documents. . . .
>
> I was soon to learn that a question is asked, you start to answer, you are interrupted by another committeeman. This happened too often to be an accident.[15]

The Bishop faced the extraordinarily difficult task of dispelling shadows. He sought to clear up what the committee calls a "file"—a hodgepodge of unverified and unevaluated "information" culled from newspaper clippings, letterheads, programs, and tidbits of "testimony" from witnesses uninhibited by any obligation to face their victim or submit to the test of cross-examination. The committee releases the contents of such files to favored citizens, organizations, and members of Congress, disclaiming any responsibility for them and insisting that the material does not represent an opinion or a conclusion of the committee. The *Washington Post* obtained a copy of the file on Bishop Oxnam, submitted it to him for comment, and on April 5, 1953, published the file in full (except for a summary condensation of one newspaper article), together with the Bishop's point-by-point reply. Since

[15] G. Bromley Oxnam, *I Protest* (New York: Harper & Brothers, 1954), pp. 22–23.

the Bishop, in the entire course of his ten-hour appearance before the committee, never had a chance to deal with the file itself, it may be useful to present here two or three sample items from its contents along with his remarks concerning them. They will help to show the caliber of the committee's work.

Item No. 1 of the file, as reproduced in the *Washington Post*, is as follows:

The *Washington Star* of February 10, 1930, carries a news item datelined Indiana State Reformatory, February 9. The article refers to a speech made by Dr. G. Bromley Oxnam, president of DePauw University, to the inmates of the reformatory. Dr. Oxnam is reported as decrying the practice of nations in entering into secret treaties, and declaring that the slogan of "America First" must be interpreted as meaning America first in world service, and not "to be the first to go to Mexico to steal oil lands."

Bishop Oxnam made the following comment on this item:

I did deliver an address at the Indiana State Reformatory, entitled "International Understanding as a Basis for World Peace." It was delivered at a time, if I recall correctly, when the oil issue in Mexico was current and the question of using military force was being discussed.

The important thing in this connection is that this paragraph should not be in the files of the committee; there is no reference here to any subversive organization. Nor is there any subversive idea expressed. My statement will stand moral scrutiny and is in keeping with the best traditions of this land.

Item No. 6:

The *Daily Worker* of September 24, 1937 (page 6), contains an article about a meeting to be held at Madison Square Garden on October 1. This meeting, held under the auspices of the American League Against War and Fascism and the American Friends of the Chinese People, featured William E. Dodd as the speaker. The name of Bishop G. Bromley Oxnam appears as a sponsor of the meeting.

Comment on Item No. 6:

I was unaware that the *Daily Worker* is to be regarded as competent testimony. I never belonged to the American League Against War and Fascism nor to the American Friends of the Chinese People. I never sponsored any meeting under the auspices of these organizations. I was fundamentally opposed to the whole idea of the so-called "United Front" and at exactly the time when it enjoyed greatest support. A column of mine, reproduced elsewhere with this article and entitled, "United Front, a Menace," must make it perfectly clear that I could not have cooperated and did not cooperate with such an agency.

Item No. 10 reads, in part:

A call to the Congress of American-Soviet Friendship, to be held November 6–8, 1943, reflects the name of Bishop G. Bromley Oxnam as a sponsor of that congress.

The Bishop's comment, in part:

On November 8, 1942, I addressed a Boston meeting known as "Salute to Our Russian Ally." Among the sponsors were Secretary and Mrs. Cordell Hull, Lord and Lady Halifax, Secretary and Mrs. Jesse Jones, Mr. and Mrs. Edward Stettinius, Jr., Major George Fielding Eliot, William Green, Robert A. Millikan, Owen D. Young, and, if I may say so, to cap the climax, Senator Kenneth McKellar. There were also distinguished leaders of religion such as the Right Reverend Henry Knox Sherrill. Frankly, I thought I was in good company.

In March 1943, I believe I agreed to serve as sponsor for a Madison Square Garden meeting of the National Council of American-Soviet Friendship. . . . I believed that we ought to give the fullest cooperation to cementing Russian-American Friendship since Russia was our ally in a war in which our very life was at stake. I might point out that both of my sons were in the Army.

These are not atypical excerpts from the file. Other items identify the Bishop with organizations to which he never belonged or note his membership, as though there were something sinister about it, in such reputable and useful organizations as the American Civil Liberties Union. There is a persistent disregard of the time factor—for instance, in regard to the National Council of American-Soviet Friendship, which he supported in 1942 and 1943; but in April 1944 he declined to accept membership on its board of directors. Nothing in the file, not a single item, reflects the slightest discredit upon him. Nothing in it affords the slightest indication that he ever had any sympathy whatever for communism or that he was ever in any way naïve or unwary about it.

In short, nothing in this file gives the slightest justification for compiling it.

The effect, if not the purpose, of such a file is intimidation. It says to the young clergyman who may hope to become the Bishop of Washington twenty years from now that he had better not join anything, or lend his name to anything, or say anything, or do anything that may, after some change in the climate of opinion, be construed as unorthodox by a committee of Congress. It says this, of course, not only to young clergymen but to every young man and woman. And its impact is to inhibit the free growth and interplay of the voluntary associations which have been the arteries of American political and social progress. It is as un-American as a Commissariat of Public Enlightenment and Culture. In the special case of a clergyman, moreover, it amounts to something very like a policing of the church by the state.

But to return to Bishop Oxnam's public catechizing by the committee. "It was apparent as the day progressed," he remarked in his book about his experience, "that the committee had no intention of dealing with the files, as such. Again and again, I urged them to come to the specific questions that I had raised. New material had been dug up, probably in the hope that I might be made ridiculous in public and the committee thereby exonerated." [16]

Instead of discussing the contents of the file on which Bishop Oxnam had asked to be heard, the committee insisted on questioning him concerning his relationships with other clergymen who, in its opinion, had strayed from the fold. The Bishop, as a witness, could only answer questions; he had no means of directing the discussion or selecting topics. In consequence, he found himself always on the defensive and often under circumstances that were extremely trying. He was forced, for example, into talking about the Reverend Harry F. Ward, who had been his teacher when Bishop Oxnam was a student at the Boston University School of Theology in 1914. Professor Ward, one of the great liberal and inspirational leaders of the Methodist Church and, at

[16] Ibid., p. 37.

one time, long ago, the head of the American Civil Liberties Union, has been a favorite whipping boy of the Committee on Un-American Activities. A member of the committee, Representative Kit Clardy of Michigan, addressing Dr. Oxnam, characterized Dr. Ward in the following terms. The form of address employed by this congressman to one distinguished minister and the sneering condemnation of another are worth noting.

> I have mentioned repeatedly, Witness, the testimony which is about to be released. I want to direct your attention to one portion of it, that portion which specifically says that when the Communist party was organized in 1919, Dr. Ward was already a convinced Communist, with a few insignificant, minor reservations. I am quoting verbatim from the testimony by Benjamin Gitlow, who was one of the founders and organizers of the Communist party in the United States. . . . I ask you to read that particularly, because you will discover through all that time of your association with him he was a Communist.

This easy acceptance of an unverified accusation by a former Communist, this bland disregard of Dr. Ward's denial that he had ever been a member of the Communist party, this sleazy implication that Dr. Oxnam was in some manner tainted by having studied for the ministry under Dr. Ward forty years earlier—these are measures of the committee's qualifications for judgment.

Bishop Oxnam testified to the affection and esteem he had felt for Professor Ward in his student days; but he felt obliged to say that he had broken with Professor Ward when the latter's views, as Dr. Oxnam believed, had shifted. They had not seen each other for many years. Thus, in some measure, perhaps, Bishop Oxnam found himself helping the committee in its efforts to discredit Professor Ward.

Similarly, when he was questioned about his relations with the Methodist Federation for Social Action and its controversial former executive secretary, the Reverend Jack R. McMichael, Bishop Oxnam found himself contributing to the public destruction of the man's reputation. He was asked, "Do you know Jack Mc-Michael?—do you know him to be a member of the Communist party?" To this the Bishop replied, "I did not know that he was a member of the Communist party, but I found myself in such fundamental opposition to Jack McMichael that I had to face one of two decisions, either to stay in and get him out or to get out myself, and it seemed to me wiser to resign and sever all relations because I was a little fearful it would take a bit longer to get him out than I had time to give." He admitted to the committee that he had received confidential information which had made him suspicious of McMichael. In other cases, too, Bishop Oxnam was pulled by the undertow of self-defense into dissociating himself from accused individuals in ways that were necessarily damaging to them.

Certainly the Bishop's appearance before the committee yielded some beneficial results. It had the virtue of exposing the shabbiness of the committee's techniques and the bad manners of its members. It produced, throughout the country, a wave of popular and editorial indignation over the presumptuousness of calling an eminent churchman to account in this fashion. The valor and skill of Bishop Oxnam's behavior won widespread acclaim. And to some extent, perhaps, Americans began to realize dimly the implications of this kind of intrusion of the state into affairs of the church.

The Bishop himself had had serious misgivings about asking for a hearing. Some of his friends had said to him, "Do not dignify them by such a request. You will be admitting the right of the state to catechize the church. Your presence may open the door to further inroads upon the principle of the separation of state and church." [17] Recalling, in his subsequent account of his experience before the committee, a series of questions put to him concerning a book that had been sent to Methodist ministers by order of the Administrative Committee of the Board of Missions and Church Extension of the Methodist Church, he concluded, "I should have informed this committee that this matter was none of its business." And it may be, indeed, that this is precisely what he should have informed the committee about the whole of its outrageous file. There is something deeply disquieting about the

[17] Ibid., p. 13.

spectacle of a bishop soliciting the vindication of a secular authority for lawful activities entered into in good faith and good conscience.

Invasion of "the shrine of conscience and private judgment" in respect to clergymen is no worse, of course, than in respect to laymen. It is merely more conspicuous. It raises, however, a collateral question of some consequence. Although ordination does not confer upon a minister any special immunity from the authority of Congress, does it not impose upon him a special obligation to resist that authority when it is misdirected? Ordination means something more than a license to perform marriages and other religious rites; it means consecration to certain values and ideals. And so, perhaps, it demands of those who have accepted it special courage and special steadfastness.

It may well be that the present use of the congressional investigating power to invade "the shrine of conscience and private judgment" can be checked only by challenge. From whom, then, is the challenge to come? Bishop Oxnam, by his appearance at a public hearing, challenged the committee in the way that he thought best. But members of the clergy in general and the churches as collective bodies have done little to rally in resistance or to evoke protest among their parishioners. Perhaps the church could make no greater contribution to the society of which it is a part than to take the lead in fixing frontiers for the authority of the state.

IV

The word "university" seems to evoke in the minds of some congressional investigators a romantic image. They like to think of a university as a place where ivied walls shelter white-thatched, absent-minded dons who converse in Sanskrit, with perhaps a few unworldly researchers puttering about a physics laboratory, concocting hydrogen bombs, but without a thought or care, of course, as to the use that more practical men may make of them. In this idyllic sanctuary, docile and trusting students gambol in from football fields, ripe for subversion by any Communist and ready to cast aside all fealty to private enterprise at the mere mention of Karl Marx.

But a university is, by definition, a place embracing a variety of disciplines, a variety of points of view. The members of its faculty have the same right as other citizens to participate in political affairs—and perhaps a special obligation to do so, deriving from their special knowledge. As educated men they tend, naturally, to take an interest in contemporary problems. And if they are good teachers, doing their part to produce good citizens, they encourage their students to take such an interest too. No university worthy of the name is isolated or insulated from the society it serves. The life of a good university is not cloistered. At its best it is full of turbulence, illuminating the problems of the present with an understanding of the past, fostering no orthodoxy but providing a forum for the expression of divergent and conflicting doctrines, encouraging men to test ideas by exposing them to intellectual competition, prompting students to use knowledge as a tool for asking questions and formulating independent thought.

The university is an instrumentality of society, not of the state. It espouses no doctrine and champions no philosophy. One of its functions is the propagation of unorthodoxy—that is, of critical thinking. Its real business is to produce men and women who will question inherited values and challenge constituted authority. For only men and women who examine and test what is passed on to them can come to a mature and stable acceptance of their heritage; and enduring loyalty comes only from those whose consent to authority is freely given. "Prove all things; hold fast that which is good," admonished St. Paul.

"There are persons in this country," observed Professor John L. Mothershead, Jr., of Stanford University, "who speak as if they wanted to produce American robots who could safely be granted civil liberties because their minds would be limited to ideas certified as safe by various investigative committees and censors at the federal, state, county, and community levels. These persons do not seem to understand that what they advocate is really a complete spiritual capitulation to communism." [18]

The notion that universities should serve the state is essentially a Communist notion. Government control of universities is an identifying characteristic of every totalitarian system. Institutions of learning, if they are free, are always a threat to tyranny. The men who met in Philadelphia in 1787 to establish a great republic relied upon such institutions to serve as a vital element in the system of checks and balances they contrived to keep governmental authority within appropriate bounds. Manifestly, universities can discharge this responsibility only if they remain genuinely independent of governmental control.

The importance of such independence has been recognized in the whole structure of American education—in the tax-supported public schools and state universities as well as in the private academies and endowed institutions. The management of public-school systems has always been a jealously guarded local concern entrusted to boards of education, democratically elected as a rule, within each county or municipality. Federal supervision in any form has been stubbornly resisted; even proposals to grant federal financial aid have been looked at askance lest such aid lead to some measure of federal interference.

Similarly, there has been an effort to protect state universities from political influences. While state legislatures, through control of appropriations, have often intruded in university affairs, the direction of the great state institutions has been left in the main to self-governing boards of regents made up of outstanding citizens. And again, federal intervention of any sort has been forbidden. The land-grant colleges, which had their inception in a subsidy from the nation, have also been kept strictly under local control.

But it has no doubt been precisely in their relative immunity from political interference that the endowed private colleges and universities have found their principal advantage over state in-

[18] *Educational Record,* quarterly journal of the American Council on Education, January 1953.

stitutions. The founders of the American Republic conceived it to be a responsibility of government to encourage education as an indispensable element of a democratic society, but not to control it. Thus the Massachusetts Constitution of 1780 provided that "it shall be the duty of legislators and magistrates, in all future periods of this commonwealth, to cherish the interests of literature and the sciences, and all seminaries of them; especially the university at Cambridge, public schools and grammar schools in the towns; to encourage private societies and public institutions." [19]

By and large, the boards of trustees and boards of regents which have governed American colleges and universities—those supported by public funds and those supported by private endowments and contributions—have been sober, conscientious, and reasonably capable bodies, in no need whatever of congressional supervision. The Americans who make up these boards are no less patriotic and no less concerned about preserving the American way of life than the Americans who make up the Congress of the United States. They are no less hostile to communism and no less devoted to free enterprise. Moreover, being outside the Congress of the United States, their judgment in regard to the affairs of the institutions they serve is much less likely to be swayed by partisan or other political considerations.

The whole thrust of contemporary congressional investigation into "Subversive Influence in the Educational Process" is, patently, an indictment of these boards. It implies that educational authorities have been lax and incompetent, that they have permitted subversive influences to become rampant and lack the wit or resolution to deal with these influences effectively on their own responsibility. The inescapable effect of the kind of congressional investigation that has been conducted by the Senate Internal Security Subcommittee is to replace, in part, the rule of independent governing bodies with the authority of the national legislature. It amounts, in plain fact, to a direct extension of

[19] Quoted by A. Whitney Griswold, Baccalaureate Address, Yale University, June 7, 1953.

federal authority into the field of education, and it operates in a crucial way to corrupt the independence of American institutions of learning—to destroy the indispensable condition of their social utility.

Like the House Un-American Activities Committee's investigation of clergymen, which disclaimed any intention of investigating the churches, the Senate Internal Security Subcommittee has concerned itself with teachers while disclaiming any thought of investigating education. But what the subcommittee's efforts come down to is nothing more nor less than a purge of the teaching profession. The subcommittee has its own standards of qualification for teaching and undertakes to measure, judge, and confirm or condemn individuals in the teaching posts to which they were appointed by non-governmental authorities.

It is of the essence of academic freedom that the qualifications of teachers be determined by their professional colleagues in accordance with professional standards. There is no other way to assure competence among them, for only their colleagues are equipped to make a satisfactory judgment on this score. And there is no other way to assure teachers of the security of tenure they must enjoy if they are to be free to teach the truth as they understand it. Teachers who use their classrooms for propaganda purposes or who distort their subjects demonstrate incompetence and violate the accepted rules of tenure. Their colleagues can be counted upon to dismiss them or otherwise discipline them for such misconduct when it has been proved after a fair hearing. But to subject them to any political test or to threaten them with political censure from the outside is to silence and shackle them. Men in fear that they may lose their jobs for unorthodox opinions or unconventional associations cannot teach freely.

Academic freedom, it should be noted, is not a privilege or indulgence extended to teachers for their idle enjoyment. It is an indispensable means of assuring society that teachers will be able to fulfill their vital function conscientiously. The preservation of it is a public, not merely a professional, interest. For this reason it needs to be jealously guarded against interference by the state. Congressional investigation of teachers—at least in the form in which it has been undertaken by the Senate Internal Security Subcommittee—is direct and disastrous interference.

"Our purpose," said Senator Jenner, who became chairman of the Internal Security Subcommittee in 1953, "is to protect and safeguard academic freedom. . . . Our committee is not concerned with telling the leaders of our schools and colleges what to teach, or how to teach. It is concerned with showing them where this alien conspiracy is hidden, that it is fully armed with every weapon, waiting to attack at every vantage point. It is concerned with helping our academic leaders to meet the threat. There can be no academic freedom until this Soviet conspiracy hidden in our schools and colleges is exposed to the light, and the rule of Moscow over its adherents in the educational world is broken." [20] One need not question the sincerity of this statement to doubt its wisdom.

Senator Jenner's premise deserves examination. While there is little doubt that the Soviet conspiracy would like to infiltrate and control American education and may be "waiting to attack at every vantage point," there is nothing to show that it is enjoying any present success. In the depression years of the 1930s, and in the war years of the 1940s when Russia was an ally of the United States, a number of teachers (hardly a great number in relation to the whole of the profession) joined the Communist party transiently, in the main for what they considered idealistic and altogether non-conspiratorial reasons. By the 1950s, before the Jenner Subcommittee ever embarked on its program of "helping our academic leaders to meet the threat," these teachers had largely left the party in disillusionment. Assuming that a few remain, the threat that they pose can hardly be called formidable, and academic leaders are quite capable of meeting it by their own tested techniques. If it is true that Communists are subject to an iron discipline and are required to serve Soviet purposes, violation of the trust reposed in them must show in their teaching and in their relations with students. It is then subject to detection and

[20] Senate Internal Security Subcommittee Report, July 17, 1953, p. 2.

discipline by school administrators and colleagues zealous to maintain the integrity of their calling. If a teacher's membership in the Communist party does not distort his performance of his academic obligations, it cannot be much of a menace.

The Jenner Subcommittee has never undertaken to show any dereliction on the part of teachers in the performance of their academic duties. It has undertaken, rather, "to expose secret members of the Communist network by its power to administer oaths and by its power of subpoena and its power to punish for contempt of Congress." [21] It adopted a policy of "welcoming the testimony of all responsible ex-Communists." [22] With this testimony as a basis, it called before it in executive session teachers accused of having once been party members. A large number of these, claiming the protection of the Fifth Amendment, refused to answer questions as to present or past membership in the party. Some denied present membership but pleaded the Fifth Amendment respecting membership in the past. Others denied having been members at any time. As a general, though not invariable, practice, the subcommittee excused from open testimony accused persons "who admitted their former Communist membership, and gave evidence, by answering questions, of their willingness to take a position against the Communist organization." [23] The subcommittee also regularly excused from open testimony those who denied past and present Communist-party membership in executive hearings. Those who pleaded the Fifth Amendment in the executive sessions, however, and those who declined to answer questions on grounds of conscience, were compelled to do it all over again, publicly, in open hearings. In these cases the subcommittee used the open hearings as a form of punishment.

The Jenner Subcommittee, it should be acknowledged, was far more mannerly and far more considerate of the witnesses called before it than, say, the McCarthy Subcommittee. It showed a good deal of dignified calm and even courtesy to a few witnesses

21 Ibid., p. 2.
22 Ibid., p. 3.
23 Ibid., p. 4.

who denounced it intemperately, asserting "rights" the subcommittee did not recognize. The conduct of some witnesses was exasperatingly evasive and unbecoming to teachers. Nevertheless, the subcommittee's practice of exposing Fifth Amendment pleaders presents a delicate question of law, which was raised pointedly by an attorney for the University of Chicago, Albert E. Jenner, Jr. (not to be confused with Senator Jenner, the subcommittee chairman).

On the morning of June 8, 1953, the subcommittee heard, in executive session, ten witnesses, members of the University of Chicago faculty. Three of these admitted past Communist-party membership, but because they answered all questions they were excused. Three denied Communist-party membership, and the subcommittee accepted their denials; they asked to be allowed to testify publicly but the request was refused. The remaining four, who invoked the privilege against self-incrimination, were required to come back before the subcommittee in the afternoon and the following day for a public hearing. Mr. Jenner, acting as their counsel, asked, "Doesn't the holding of a public hearing and the selection of these four men out of the ten who testified this morning impair their privilege under the Fifth Amendment?" [24] The subcommittee evidently thought not. A few minutes later Jenner raised the question again, observing that "the committee has already ascertained that these four men are invoking the Fifth Amendment privilege, and to require them to invoke it in public session, the committee having already ascertained all it can ascertain from these witnesses, is a violation of their constitutional rights." [25]

Whatever the merits of the constitutional question, the effect of the subcommittee's practice was to treat invoking of the Fifth Amendment as though it amounted to an admission of guilt. Moreover, it lumped together indiscriminately those who invoked the privilege respecting present as well as past party membership

[24] Hearings on "Subversive Influence in the Educational Process," Part 12, p. 1077.
[25] Ibid., p. 1079.

and those who invoked it respecting the past only, having denied membership in the present. The effect was also to jeopardize the jobs of these witnesses.

A teacher who appears before the Jenner Subcommittee and is questioned about past Communist-party membership finds himself impaled on one or another of the prongs of a trident. If he denies having been a party member, he runs the risk of a perjury prosecution based on testimony identifying him as a former Communist by one or another of the former—and professedly reformed —Communists tapped by the subcommittee. If he admits past membership, asserting that he has left the party, he runs the risk of being required to name persons who were associated with him when he belonged—a kind of degradation that any sensitive man may desire to escape. If he refuses to answer the question at all, pleading the constitutional privilege against self-incrimination, the subcommittee will "expose" him in a deliberate effort to have his university dismiss him.

By and large, universities have displayed an almost eager willingness to cooperate with the subcommittee. In its report of July 17, 1953, the subcommittee was able to announce that "in all but a few of the cases before the subcommittee, the university officials and local authorities suspended the teachers who invoked their privilege against incrimination when asked about Communist-party membership. The following universities suspended faculty members therefor: Rutgers, Brooklyn Polytechnical Institute, Columbia, Vermont, New York University, Queens, Hunter, City College of New York, and Brooklyn." [26] Indeed, in all save a few institutions of higher learning, suspension or summary dismissal has become an automatic and indiscriminate reaction to a Fifth Amendment plea.

This received encouragement and oblique endorsement from a statement issued March 24, 1953, by the Association of American Universities, comprising the presidents of a number of America's greatest academic institutions. After a rather eloquent declaration about the nature of a university and its need for independence

[26] Senate Internal Security Subcommittee Report, p. 14.

—including the assertion that "so long as an instructor's observations are scholarly and germane to his subject, his freedom of expression in his classroom should not be curtailed"—the association enunciated the following views regarding the Fifth Amendment:

> As in all acts of association, the professor accepts conventions which become morally binding. Above all, he owes his colleagues in the university complete candor and perfect integrity, precluding any kind of clandestine or conspiratorial activities. He owes equal candor to the public. If he is called upon to answer for his convictions it is his duty as a citizen to speak out. It is even more definitely his duty as a professor. Refusal to do so, on whatever legal grounds, cannot fail to reflect upon a profession that claims for itself the fullest freedom to speak and the maximum protection of that freedom available in our society. In this respect, invocation of the Fifth Amendment places upon a professor a heavy burden of proof of his fitness to hold a teaching position and lays upon his university an obligation to re-examine his qualifications for membership in its society.

Perhaps the best comment on this position—although expressed in a context quite apart from it—was made by Professor Clark Byse of the University of Pennsylvania Law School:

> The automatic-dismissal approach violates the basic principle of academic freedom, that a teacher who has earned a tenure status shall be removed from his position only if he has been found to be incompetent, has been convicted of a serious crime, or has been guilty of such grave moral delinquencies as unfit him for association with students. There can be no doubt that, however much one may deplore the widespread use of the Fifth Amendment, the exercise of this constitutional privilege is not in every instance an indication either of criminality or moral delinquency. Nor is it a reflection on the witness's competence as a teacher.
>
> The proper exercise of the privilege is, instead, the result of a choice made within the limits of the law. The fact that one may wish that the choice had been otherwise is irrelevant. For it is exactly that freedom to follow one's own conscience within the law which is the essence of academic freedom. Yet, if it is proper for university administrators and trustees to impose their moral code on teachers in this respect, it is difficult to see why they may not do so in other instances. The automatic discharge of teachers for the legitimate exercise of a constitutional

privilege thus can become the precedent for other invasions of academic freedom. Purges once begun know no stopping place. [27]

There is an additional, and perhaps even more compelling, consideration to be taken into account here. It is nothing less than an outright abdication of academic independence for any university to serve indiscriminately as the executor of punishments arbitrarily imposed by a congressional committee. To discipline teachers automatically for a lawful refusal to cooperate with a committee of Congress is to put into the hands of that committee a formidable device for determining the membership of university faculties—something which ought to be determined by the faculties themselves. If the colleges and universities of the United States allow this system of selection to go on, they will have effectively shifted the fulcrum of control from their own authority to the authority of the government. Academic freedom can prevail only in institutions of learning that are genuinely self-governing.

In striking contrast to the policy of automatic dismissal, Harvard University furnished a demonstration of independence, responsibility, and thoughtful discrimination in dealing with three faculty members who resorted to the Fifth Amendment, one of them in an appearance before the Velde Committee of the House, the other two before the Jenner Subcommittee. Harvard announced a principle "that no general rule will be applied in cases in which members of our teaching staff invoke the Fifth Amendment, but that each case will be decided on its merits after full and deliberate consideration of the facts and issues involved." [28] The three faculty members were interviewed by a committee of the Harvard Corporation and were given a hearing before the full corporation, which studied the transcript of their appearances before the congressional bodies and conferred on their cases with a faculty advisory committee.

The corporation came to the conclusion that none of them was

[27] Clark Byse, "Teachers and the Fifth Amendment," *University of Pennsylvania Law Review*, Vol. 102, No. 7 (May 1954).
[28] Statement by the Harvard Corporation in regard to Associate Professor Wendell H. Furry, Teaching Fellow Leon J. Kamin, and Assistant Professor Helen Deane Markham, May 20, 1953.

at that time a Communist-party member, that their teaching had been altogether satisfactory and untainted by Communist indoctrination, that they had at no time, in or out of class, attempted to influence the political thinking of their students. The corporation expressed regret that the three teachers had not seen fit to tell their stories candidly to the committees and regarded this failure as "misconduct which creates the necessity for us to inquire into the full facts." It found one of the faculty members guilty of grave misconduct and placed him on probation for three years because its inquiry disclosed that he had falsely told an investigating agent in 1944 that he had no reason to believe an applicant for classified government work had been a member of the Communist party. The corporation concluded that the other two faculty members had not been guilty of grave misconduct and that it would take no disciplinary action against them.[29]

Sarah Lawrence College faced a somewhat different problem and handled it with equal independence. Irving Goldman, an anthropologist on its faculty since 1947, was called before the Jenner Subcommittee in executive session in March 1953. He testified frankly that he had been a member of the Communist party prior to 1942, had left it in that year, and had had no association with it since. He refused, however, on moral grounds and without invoking the Fifth Amendment, to name persons he had known to be fellow-members. On April 1, 1953, he was called before a public session of the subcommittee and recited again the details of his own rather uneventful career as a Communist. But when he was asked to tell the names of members of the unit he had belonged to at Columbia University, where he had served in the mid-1930s as an assistant in anthropology, he answered, "I am sorry, as I told you and the committee in executive session, I cannot as a matter of principle reveal those names."

MR. MORRIS (counsel to the subcommittee): What is the principle that you mentioned then?

[29] The Senate subsequently voted contempt citations against two of the three, Messrs. Furry and Kamin, for refusal to answer certain questions put to them by the McCarthy Subcommittee in later hearings.

MR. GOLDMAN: The principle, I think, is a simple one, which is that I cannot inform on others to get others into trouble, particularly since I have no knowledge that any of these individuals had ever committed any offense against the security of the United States. So far as I know, they had violated no law.

SENATOR WELKER (presiding): That is about the best reason why you could answer it then, is it not?

MR. GOLDMAN: Well, sir, if I may explain again, I believe this would be getting a lot of people into trouble, and I want to say I have come here to speak very frankly about myself; I have made no appeal to any legal immunities, and I simply cannot allow to rest on my conscience that I would get other people into trouble just to save myself some difficulty.[30]

Warned by Senator Herman Welker of Idaho that the subcommittee would seek a contempt citation against him, and ordered by him to answer the questions, Goldman said simply: "My statement is that with all due respect to the Senate of the United States, I must still stand upon my principles, and I would like to add further that the principle isn't worth standing on unless there is a problem in standing upon it. The fact that I am under fire is no reason for abandoning a principle. . . . I think in a matter of this kind a person must rest upon his own conscience. I could not in all conscience leave this committee room with the knowledge that I had gotten other people into trouble to save myself."[31]

It would be a strange view of academic freedom that could find grounds for disciplining a teacher for this forthright reliance on conscience and principle. The Board of Trustees of Sarah Lawrence College, after reviewing the record and conferring with the appropriate faculty committees and with President Taylor and Dean Raushenbush, concluded that Goldman, in refusing to name former associates in the Communist party "did so on the basis of his personal standard of fair dealing and not for the purpose of defying the committee. This called for no action by the Board of Trustees. The reports as to his character and teach-

[30] Senate Internal Security Subcommittee Hearings, Part 6, p. 735.
[31] Ibid., p. 737.

ing showed that he was qualified to continue as a member of the faculty of Sarah Lawrence College." [32]

The stature of Harvard University and of Sarah Lawrence College was surely not diminished by their insistence on making their own judgment, independently, as to the fitness of members of their faculties. Such independence is the one unforsakable condition of academic freedom. Where it exists, there flows through the faculty an invigorating sense that the institution will stand behind them so long as they do their jobs competently and conscientiously, that they will be judged on the basis of present performance by men who understand the nature and conditions of their work, and not on the basis of past political vagaries by men ignorant of academic standards and indifferent to them. Where such independence is relinquished, fear prevails.

The evil impact of congressional investigation of teachers—and of complacent acceptance of such investigation by academic authorities—is that, however loftily it is motivated and however legally it is justified, it makes men wary. Particularly at the level of higher learning, where challenge and discussion ought to be uninhibited, it puts leashes on men's minds. It leads men to measure what they say in terms of its acceptability to the government. It builds walls about the universities, isolating them from society, because it tells teachers that it is safer and shrewder for them to refrain from all extracurricular activities and all participation in the problems of the society. This is the blight that has fallen upon the universities behind what we like to call the Iron Curtain. It is a dismal paradox that it should be extended to the universities of the United States in the name of anti-communism.

The justification of any governmental activity must lie in the service it renders to society. It may well be that some of the witnesses who squirmed and wriggled under the interrogation of the Reece, Velde, and Jenner committees were Communists. Cer-

[32] Statement to the Students, Faculty, and Alumnae Council from the Board of Trustees of Sarah Lawrence College, April 21, 1953.

tainly a number of them had been Communists at some time in their careers. But was the discomfiture of these individuals worth the cost that it entailed in terms of setting an official standard of conformity before men whose work demands of them a high degree of nonconformity? Were the benefits of these investigations commensurate with the dangers involved in the extension of governmental authority into areas of association, conscience, and expression? Did the inquiries, in fact, serve any legitimate legislative purpose?

One witness, Miss Robenia F. Anthony, who appeared before the Jenner Subcommittee in hearings held at Boston, Massachusetts, asked a pertinent question which the subcommittee has never satisfactorily answered. After she had been sworn and seated, the following exchange, reproduced verbatim from the printed record of the hearing, took place between Miss Anthony and Robert Morris, the subcommittee counsel:

MR. MORRIS: Miss Anthony, have you been a teacher in your lifetime?

MISS ANTHONY: I have taught for forty-seven years, and I have been retired for five years.

MR. MORRIS: Now, will you tell us, Miss Anthony, where you have been doing your teaching and in what schools?

MISS ANTHONY: All those forty-seven years? Well, I mean, I can tell you it. I was forty-three years in Springfield. When I began, I began in a little country school in the Berkshires, in Washington, and then from Washington my superintendent promoted me to Warren, and I taught in Warren; and then after Warren I taught in—let's see—after Warren where did I teach? I think I taught in Hingham and Holliston. I taught in all those places, but I have been in Springfield forty-three years, and I have not been connected with the system for five years in June—it will be five years.

Can you people hear me all right?

MR. MORRIS: Yes.

(Laughter from the audience.)

THE CHAIRMAN: This is a courtroom. This is a judicial proceeding of the committee. Please, please hold down the laughter and amusement, or we'll have to clear the courtroom.

MR. MORRIS: Now, have you ever attended a national convention of the Communist party?

MISS ANTHONY: Now, I'll have to state this fact: That I believe thoroughly in political and academic freedom. I have always stood up for that. I believe it as thoroughly as I believe in the Constitution of the United States, and I cannot go back on the principles of a long life-time.

I'm almost seventy-four now, and to go back just before my death on the principles that I have stood for all my life, I can't do it, so I'll have to respectfully ask you people if I can decline to answer that on account of not wanting to testify against myself and others under the Fifth Amendment.

THE CHAIRMAN: Well, the committee recognizes your refusal to answer under the Fifth Amendment—

MISS ANTHONY: Then I don't need to—

THE CHAIRMAN: But denies any other reasons.

MISS ANTHONY: Excuse me. I felt I ought to let you know it wasn't lack of cooperation, but it was a heartfelt, honest desire on my part to die as consistently as I have tried to live. . . .

She was asked a number of other questions bearing on the same subject and declined to answer almost all of them on the same grounds. Then, when the chairman said there would be no further questions, the hearing came to a close as follows:

MISS ANTHONY: Would you like to have me read a little short sentence that I've written, a little short statement I have?

THE CHAIRMAN: You can submit it to the committee.

MISS ANTHONY to the committee: You don't want to take the time to hear it. It won't take longer than a minute, gentlemen.

THE CHAIRMAN: Do you want it to be put in the record or read it?

MISS ANTHONY: Do you mind if I read it, because I did take the trouble to write it, you know.

THE CHAIRMAN: All right.

MISS ANTHONY: This is my fifth year of retirement after forty-seven years of teaching in Massachusetts, forty-three in Springfield.

And, to save your arithmetic, it makes me seventy-four years old.

I have helped hundreds of pupils to become responsible citizens and to think and base their conclusions on adequate facts and then to act on those conclusions.

From the days when I helped organize the teachers' division of woman suffrage marchers here and up Beacon Street, I have tried to be an honest thinker and a worker for civil liberties, academic and political freedom.

For several years I was vice-president of the central labor union, the only woman who has attained that honor and a position that I kept until I retired.

When I invoke the Fifth Amendment, I do it to protect myself and other guiltless people from incrimination and even the possibility of future harassing prosecution.

Thus, after a long and honorable life as a good teacher, I find myself questioned here in the investigation of a school system with which I have had no connection for almost five years. I just say, "Why?" (Applause from the audience.)

(Witness excused.)

CHAPTER VIII

CONGRESS AND
THE FOURTH ESTATE

The greatest tyranny has the smallest beginning. From precedents
overlooked, from remonstrances despised, from grievances treated with
ridicule, from powerless men oppressed with impunity, and overbearing men tolerated with complacence, springs the tyrannical usage
which generations of wise and good men may hereafter perceive and
lament and resist in vain. At present, common minds no more see a
crushing tyranny in trivial unfairness or ludicrous indignity, than the
eye uninformed by reason can discern the sap in the acorn, or the utter
desolation of winter in the first autumnal fall. Hence the necessity of
denouncing with unwearied and even troublesome perseverance a
single act of oppression. Let it alone and it stands on record. The country has allowed it and when it is at last provoked to a late indignation,
it finds itself gagged with the record of its own ill compulsion.[1]

I

THE PRESS is, in many respects, the most privileged of American institutions. Although newspapers are big-business enterprises operated for private profit, and although they are in some
degree subsidized by the government through the grant of second-
class mail benefits, the Constitution of the United States guaran-
tees them an almost absolute immunity from governmental regu-

[1] *The Times* (London), August 11, 1846, quoted by John Jewkes, *Ordeal
by Planning* (New York: The Macmillan Co., 1948).

lation. And this constitutional guarantee is buttressed by popular reverence and tradition. In the liturgy of American politics, "freedom of the press" is a symbol and a prime article of faith.

"Freedom of the press," in the sense in which it is guaranteed by the American Constitution, means freedom to publish without interference or restraint from the government. This right, conferred upon the press as an institution, is exercised, of course, by the individuals who happen to be the owners and managers of newspapers. They are accountable to no public authority save that which may be exerted unofficially through shifting popular prejudices and preferences. "Somebody has said quite aptly," Walter Lippmann noted in *Public Opinion*, "that the newspaper editor has to be re-elected every day." [2] It is worth remembering, however, that he is re-elected on the basis of prejudices and preferences which he has no small share in generating. And the choice of candidates is narrowly limited by economic considerations.

In no other country do publishers enjoy so full a measure of freedom. The authors of the Constitution desired a relationship between press and government, just as they desired a relationship between church and government, radically different from that existing in the England from which they declared their independence. No other conclusion can comport with their bracketing of the two in the same unequivocal language of the First Amendment. They desired to keep the press free not only from previous restraint in the form of direct censorship—a freedom already accorded it in England—but also from the fear of punishment for publishing what might be deemed offensive to the government. They desired, in short, to assure, as Professor Chafee has put it, "unrestricted discussion of public affairs." He quotes James Madison, who drafted the First Amendment, as basing his explanation of it in 1799 on "the essential difference between the British Government and the American Constitution." [3]

[2] Walter Lippmann, *Public Opinion* (New York: The Macmillan Co., 1930), p. 321.
[3] Zechariah Chafee, Jr., *Free Speech in the United States* (Cambridge: Harvard University Press, 1942), p. 19.

Recent Supreme Court interpretations of the First Amendment have uniformly held it to protect the press not only from legislative restraints but from summary punishment for contempt by the judiciary branch of the government. State courts no less than federal courts are forbidden to discipline newspapers for comment on trials unless the comment presents a clear and present danger to the administration of justice.[4] This gives newspapers in the United States a greater degree of latitude than that accorded in England. Indeed, it makes them, in a sense, inescapably irresponsible; and it should afford no occasion for surprise that some of them sometimes behave with gross irresponsibility.

Toleration of some degree of irresponsibility is an inevitable price of the freedom requisite to a discharge of the vital function of the press. Since governmental control embraces the hazard that it will become tyrannical, private control, despite its own hazards, has been accepted by the American people as preferable. As Tocqueville observed, "In order to enjoy the inestimable benefits which liberty of the press insures, it is necessary to submit to the inevitable evils which it engenders."[5]

What, then, is the vital function for the sake of which Americans grant the press so privileged a position? The men who wrote the First Amendment conceived of a wholly independent press as an indispensable device for keeping governmental authority within appropriate bounds. So far from desiring censorship of the press by the government, they sought censorship of the government by the press. This view was stated explicitly by Thomas Jefferson in a letter to President Washington in 1792: "No government ought to be without censors, and where the press is free, no one ever will." Despite all that he suffered from the abusive and irresponsible Federalist newspapers of his day, as late as 1823 he was able to write of the press to a French correspondent: "This formidable censor of the public functionaries, by arraigning them at the tribunal of public opinion, produces reform peaceably,

---

[4] *Near v. Minnesota*, 283 U.S. 697 (1931); *Bridges v. California*, 314 U.S. 252 (1941); *Pennekamp v. Florida*, 328 U.S. 331 (1946); *Craig v. Harney*, 331 U.S. 367 (1947).

[5] Tocqueville, op. cit., p. 104.

which must otherwise be done by revolution." [6] This view of the relation of the press to the government was the common sense of that time. The First Continental Congress, in an "Address to the Inhabitants of the Province of Quebec" in 1774, referred to liberty of the press as a means "whereby oppressive officers are shamed or intimidated into more honorable or just modes of conducting affairs." [7]

The Russians—indeed, all totalitarians—see this relationship differently. They view any criticism of the government as inimical to the public welfare, because they consider the government the only appropriate agent of the collective will (as that will is made manifest by the Communist party); consequently they hold that control exercised by the government is the same thing as popular control. Opposition to the government is thus equated with opposition to the people, and freedom of the press is therefore forbidden in the name of liberty and democracy. Lenin stated the Communist position with remarkable candor in 1920. "Why should freedom of speech and freedom of the press be allowed?" he asked. "Why should a government which is doing what it believes to be right allow itself to be criticized? It would not allow opposition by lethal weapons. Ideas are much more fatal things than guns. Why should any man be allowed to buy a printing press and disseminate pernicious opinions calculated to embarrass the government?"

Why, indeed? The answer has never been better expressed than by Thomas Erskine, when he was defending Thomas Paine against a libel charge in a British court two centuries ago. "In this manner," he said, "power has reasoned in every age; government *in its own estimation,* has been at all times a system of perfection; but a free press has examined and detected its errors, and the people have from time to time reformed them. This freedom has alone made our government what it is! This freedom alone can preserve it."

[6] Quoted by Frank L. Mott, *Jefferson and the Press* (Baton Rouge: Louisiana State University Press, 1943), p. 6.
[7] First Journal of the Continental Congress, containing the proceedings from September 5, 1774, to January 1, 1776, p. 61.

Macauley called the press "a fourth estate." The term connotes independence. Commenting on the position of the press in a free society, Herbert Brucker, the editor of the *Hartford Courant*, remarked illuminatingly that "all other estates of the social order . . . stand together on one side of a line, while the Fourth Estate remains on the other." [8] This separation is the essence of freedom of the press. It is the necessary condition for fulfillment of the vital function of the press. It is, perhaps, the key to every other form of freedom. "The more we consider the independence of the press in its principal consequences," said Tocqueville, "the more are we convinced that it is the chief and, so to speak, the constitutive element of freedom in the modern world. A nation which is determined to remain free is therefore right in demanding the unrestrained exercise of this independence." [9]

II

Although Congress has generally been wary of any legislation trenching on the freedom of the press, it has more than once sought to lay hands on particular newspapers through the exercise of its investigating power. The newspapers have usually rebuffed these attempts with a pretty sturdy show of independence. Individual newspapermen have resolutely refused to reveal to committees their confidential sources of information, asserting a "right" rooted more in tradition than in law, and have generally had the backing of their colleagues and publishers; in fact, their obduracy has generally made the "right" respected. In this country the history of freedom of the press, from John Peter Zenger's time to ours, has been a history of individual challenge to arbitrary authority. Perhaps it is not too much to say that this is the history of all human freedom.

Among twentieth-century challenges to the intrusion of congressional authority into newspaper affairs, one of the most nota-

[8] Herbert Brucker, *Freedom of Information* (New York: The Macmillan Co., 1949), p. 31.
[9] Tocqueville, op. cit., p. 110.

ble occurred in 1915, when a Senate committee under the chairmanship of Senator Thomas J. Walsh of Montana called the *New York Times* before it and inquired into that paper's financial backing and editorial policies. The *Times* had published editorials vigorously opposing an administration bill for the purchase of foreign ships interned in American harbors at the start of World War I. This afforded the pretext for haling two of the newspaper's executives before the committee. The chairman, it developed, had received a letter with an undecipherable signature insinuating that British interests had prompted the *Times'* editorial position. He demanded an account of the *Times'* financial backing, which was readily furnished to him, and then proceeded to a wide range of questions respecting editorial policy and news policy. Members of the committee asked the two editors, Carr Van Anda and Charles Miller, why certain stories were not put on the front page, why they had deleted certain adjectives from overseas dispatches, how much money the paper received from ship advertising, what their opinions were on a variety of current issues. All these questions were answered respectfully and patiently. At the close of the hearing, however, Mr. Miller gave the committee an opinion it had not solicited:

I can see no ethical, moral, or legal right that you have to put many of the questions you put to me today. Inquisitorial proceedings of this kind would have a very marked tendency, if continued and adopted as a policy, to reduce the press of the United States to the level of the press in some of the Central European empires, the press that has been known as the reptile press, that crawls on its belly every day to the foreign office or to the government officials and ministers to know what it may say or shall say—to receive its orders.

There was an upsurge of indignation from the press in general. Most newspapers recognized that the issue did not involve the *Times* alone but concerned, as a *Times* editorial put it, "a question of the extent to which a government's machinery may be privately misused to discredit a newspaper whose editorial attitude has become distasteful and embarrassing." The constitutional prohibition against any law abridging the freedom of the press would be rendered meaningless if newspapers could be harassed and censured at will by congressional committees for the expression of editorial opinions.

A somewhat different response to congressional inquiry was made by a Washington newspaperman, Frank C. Waldrop of the *Washington Herald,* who was subpoenaed in 1936 by the House Committee on Military Affairs. Waldrop had published a story connecting Representative John J. McSwain, a member of the committee, with some war-surplus speculators. He came to the hearing with an attorney, who stepped forward at the outset and told the committee that his client would answer no questions because the committee was proceeding improperly, "pursuant to a threat of its chairman and without legislative purpose." The American Newspaper Publishers Association, in a subsequent report, gave the following account of what occurred:

The committee, particularly its chairman, became enraged at this challenge. The chairman ordered the reporter to take the stand, administered the oath, and then asked, "Your name is Frank C. Waldrop, is it not?"

With a smile, the witness replied, "Upon the advice of counsel, I decline to answer."

Then followed one of the most disgraceful exhibitions in the history of congressional inquisitions . . . ; finally he [Waldrop] was told to stand down, but to hold himself subject to recall.

The committee proceeded for several days with its inquiry. As witness after witness gave more and more damaging testimony, its chairman became more and more embarrassed.

On April 15 a halt was called. At an executive session the committee voted unanimously to end its inquiry, not to print the record of its proceedings, and to make no report to the House.

The following day Mr. Waldrop's counsel demanded and obtained a cancellation of his subpoena.

Thus did a courageous reporter, in the face of threats, innuendo, and malicious insult, uphold the traditions of American journalism.[10]

[10] Quoted by J. R. Wiggins, *Background on Investigations of the Press,* Nieman Reports, October 1953; distributed to members of the American Society of Newspaper Editors by Mr. Wiggins, chairman of the Special Committee of the ASNE appointed to study and comment on the Wechsler hearings before the McCarthy Subcommittee.

The traditions of American journalism were equally involved in the questioning of James A. Wechsler, editor of the *New York Post,* by the McCarthy Subcommittee on Investigations. Wechsler was called before the subcommittee in executive session on April 24, 1953.[11] The chairman stated the purpose of the hearing at the outset in the following terms: "I may say the reason for your being called today is that you are one of the many authors of books whose books have been used in the information program in various libraries, and we would like to check into a number of matters." [12]

The subcommittee paid brief attention to Wechsler's books, however, and the questioning turned quickly to an altogether different subject—the personnel and editorial policies of Wechsler's newspaper. After reciting the titles of the books he had written, Wechsler was led by the subcommittee counsel, Roy Cohn, to acknowledge what was already well known and what he had never attempted to conceal—that he had joined the Young Communist League when he was eighteen years old, in his junior year at Columbia University; he managed to say also what was equally well known, that he had left the Young Communist League and the whole of the Communist movement by the end of 1937, when he was twenty-two, and had been militantly and articulately anti-Communist ever since. At that point the chairman broke into Cohn's questioning to take the discussion off on a new tack.

THE CHAIRMAN: May I interrupt, Mr. Cohn? Mr. Wechsler, do you have any other people who are members of the Young Communist League, who were or are members of the Young Communist League, working for you on your newspaper?

MR. WECHSLER: Well, Senator, I will say that I am going to answer that question, because I believe that it is a citizen's responsibility to testify before a Senate committee whether he likes the committee or not.

THE CHAIRMAN: I know you do not like this committee.

[11] At Wechsler's insistence the transcript of this hearing and of a subsequent hearing on May 5, 1953, were released to the public.
[12] Hearing before the Permanent Subcommittee on Investigations, U.S. Senate, on State Department Information Program—Information Centers, April 24, 1953, Part 4, p. 253.

MR. WECHSLER: I want to say that I think you are now exploring a subject which the American Society of Newspaper Editors might want to consider at some length.

I answer the question solely because I recognize your capacity for misstatement or misinterpretation of a failure to answer. I answer it with the protest signified.

To my knowledge, there are no Communists on the staff of the *New York Post* at this time.[13]

There followed a number of questions about the past political views and affiliations of several individuals employed by the *Post*, until Wechsler said, "Senator, may I ask at this point whether this is an investigation of me, or the *New York Post?*" Senator McCarthy answered, "It is checking the type of individuals whose books are being purchased to fight communism, allegedly." [14]

The Senator pursued his checking of the type of individuals "whose books are being purchased to fight communism, allegedly," by asking Wechsler these questions, among others:

"Have you been making attacks upon J. Edgar Hoover in the editorial columns of your paper?"

"Have you ever, in your editorial columns, over the last two years, praised the FBI?"

"Have you always been very critical of the heads of the Un-American Activities Committee? You have always thought they were pretty bad men, have you not?"

"And you are opposed to Bill Jenner, too. You think he is a dangerous man?"

"How about Velde? You are opposed to him, are you not?"

"Is there any doubt in your mind that Harry Dexter White . . . was a Communist agent?" [15]

These are, it must be acknowledged, interesting questions— questions almost any editor would ordinarily be glad to answer, perhaps even without being asked. Almost any editor would have misgivings, however, about answering them under compulsion or duress. Wechsler answered them with some asperity but more or less patiently and politely, although their pertinence to his

---

[13] Ibid., p. 256.
[14] Ibid., p. 259.
[15] Ibid., pp. 260–63 passim.

books must have seemed to him obscure. He listened while the chairman employed the authority conferred on him by the Senate to say, "I have read enough of your stuff, Mr. Wechsler, to find that your paper, as far as I know, always leads the vanguard, with the *Daily Worker*, follows the same line, against anyone who is willing to expose Communists in government." [16]

Near the close of the hearing McCarthy asked Wechsler if he felt he had been "unfairly treated." "I regard this proceeding," said the editor, "as the first in a long line of attempts to intimidate editors who do not equate McCarthyism with patriotism." [17] And after McCarthy asked him if he felt that he, personally, had been intimidated, Wechsler declared:

The *Post* has been fighting Senator McCarthy for a long time. Our editorial page, I am happy to say, has never wavered on this point. It is not going to change now, and I say again for the record that I answered freely here today because I do not believe that I have anything to hide or that the *Post* has anything to hide.

I regard this inquiry as a clear invasion of what used to be considered the newspaper's right to act and function independently. I am hopeful that there will be voices raised by newspapers throughout the country in protest against this inquiry, but I repeat again that, rather than give Senator McCarthy the opportunity to distort my stand on that principle, I have answered all questions here to the best of my knowledge and recollection.[18]

There is persuasive evidence in this statement, and indeed in Wechsler's whole demeanor, that he was not intimidated by Senator McCarthy's questioning. But he is, as he said of himself at one point in the hearing, "a pretty tough guy"; moreover, he enjoyed the security of editing a metropolitan newspaper with a publisher tough enough to back him unflinchingly. It could hardly be said with certainty that editors of other newspapers would be altogether unaffected by this hearing. It was a transparent reprisal against an editor and a newspaper for their criticism of a congressional committee and its chairman. Not every

[16] Ibid., p. 271.
[17] Ibid., p. 275.
[18] Ibid., p. 277.

editor would face with equanimity the prospect of such an experience as the price of critical comment. Not every newspaper would continue unwaveringly to oppose a chairman capable of wielding his senatorial power so punitively.

This was not in any reasonable sense of the term an inquiry calculated to help the Senate in its legislative business. It was use of the investigating power to gratify the personal vindictiveness of an individual committee chairman. This kind of browbeating—conducted under star-chamber circumstances—would seem ugly in the case of any law-abiding citizen: it has especially ominous implications in the case of a dissident newspaper editor. Official censure of editorial opinion can come pretty close to constituting a form of censorship.

There were, as Wechsler hoped, many voices raised by newspapers throughout the country in protest against this inquiry. But the American Society of Newspaper Editors—the organization to which he turned naturally and properly for the collective judgment of the American press on this infringement of its freedom— failed to recognize the significance of a senator's calling an editor to account for the editorial policies of his newspaper. The ASNE, at Wechsler's request, appointed a special committee to study his case. Its eleven members were unable to agree. The disagreement among them, they reported, "ranges from the opinion that Senator Joseph McCarthy, as committee chairman, infringed freedom of the press with his questions about the editorial policies of the *New York Post* (an opinion held by the chairman of the committee), to the contrary viewpoint that the Senator's inquiries did no damage to this freedom. In between are committee members who were disturbed by the tenor of the investigation but do not feel that this single interchange constituted a clear and present danger to freedom of the press justifying a specific challenge." [19]

Four members of the special committee submitted a minority report distinguished for its insight and eloquence. They were

[19] Comment on the Wechsler Hearings by the Special Committee of the American Society of Newspaper Editors, August 13, 1953.

J. R. Wiggins, managing editor, *Washington Post* and chairman of the committee; Herbert Brucker, editor, *Hartford Courant;* William M. Tugman, editor, *Eugene* (Oregon) *Register-Guard;* Eugene S. Pulliam, Jr., managing editor, *Indianapolis News.* They began by pointing out that "under laws made by Congress, or color thereof, Mr. Wechsler was present by compulsion and under the necessity either to answer whatever inquiries were propounded to him or face prosecution for refusal to do so. Action under these laws, or under any other laws that have been made or could be made by Congress, in abridgment of freedom of speech or of the press was barred by the inexorable command of the First Amendment." And they moved, then, to these unequivocal conclusions:

(a) Freedom of the press in these United States, as it has been understood since the adoption of the Constitution, could not long survive the repeated exercise by Congress of unlimited inquiry into the conduct of newspapers.

(b) Congressional interrogation, such as occurred in the United States Senate committee on April 24 and May 5, if frequently repeated, would extinguish, without the passage of a single law, that free and unfettered reporting of events and comment thereon, upon which the preservation of our liberties depends. . . .

(c) Newspapers put to the necessity of explaining to government agencies, legislative or executive, their news and editorial policies, under oath, would exist in such permanent jeopardy that their freedom to report fully and comment freely inevitably would be impaired. They would exist under an intimidation and harassment wholly incompatible with American ideas of liberty. . . .

(d) The people suffer some diminution of their right to know fully and comment freely upon their own government whenever a single newspaper, however worthy or unworthy, is subjected by one Senator, however worthy or unworthy, to inconvenience, expense, humiliation, ridicule, abuse, condemnation, and reproach, under the auspices of governmental power. . . .

(e) Motives of legislators and newspapermen do not alter the principles involved in any proceeding that threatens an extension of legislative power beyond those precincts within which it has been confined by the letter of the Constitution and by the spirit of our free institutions. A good Senator extinguishing the freedom of a bad newspaper may sentence generations yet unborn to a deprivation of their liberty quite as absolute as that which might flow from a bad Senator extinguishing the freedom of a good newspaper. . . . The noblest Senator that ever lived cannot interrogate the meanest editor that ever existed under the auspices of governmental power without putting in jeopardy the people's right to a free press. . . .

(f) Newspapermen, by the very choice of their profession, avail themselves of the privileges and immunities of a free press, guaranteed in the Constitution, and they assume at the same time certain obligations and duties, not the least among which is the duty to defend the freedom of the press against all attack. Where such an invasion of freedom occurs, other citizens may speak or remain silent without being identified with the trespass; but the silence of the press is invariably construed, and properly construed, as an indication that no trespass has occurred and its silences inevitably will be summoned to the support of like trespasses in the future. In our opinion, therefore, whatever inconvenience results, whatever controversy ensues, we are compelled by every command of duty to brand this and every threat to freedom of the press, from whatever source, as a peril to American freedom.

III

How well has the American press as a whole used the freedom granted to it? The harassment to which Wechsler was subjected by McCarthy is rare, and alarming chiefly as a precedent which, if left unchallenged, might become a commonplace. Newspapers criticize a great many activities of the government with a great deal of vigor and without any fear of reprisal. It is immaterial whether the criticism is captious or judicious, soundly based or ill informed. It serves to compel government officials to explain their programs and justify their decisions; and it also serves to keep the public informed about public affairs and alert to new assertions of governmental authority. It may be said, therefore, to fulfill in significant measure the first function of a free press—to act as a censor of the government.

Most newspapers have discharged their censorial duties with a good deal of bite and fervor respecting what is commonly called "corruption in the government." If the American public has remained ignorant of the scandals in federal tax collection or housing or electric-power contracts, it has not been the fault of the press, generally speaking. There has been abundant exposure of the kind of corruption that takes the form of venality. But if there is substance to the thesis of this book—that contemporary abuses of the congressional investigating power have tended to cause an imbalance among the separated branches of the government, have tended, indeed, to establish a legislative tyranny—then a kind of corruption deeper and more dangerous than venality has been taking place, a corruption of basic American values, against which much of the press has given the public no adequate warning. An expansion of governmental power has occurred, and an encroachment of that power upon traditional civil liberties of a sort that the authors of the Bill of Rights would have considered intolerable —and which they relied upon a free press to prevent.

There have been, of course, numerous press protests concerning the uglier extravagances of investigating committees. But these have been aimed, for the most part, at the bad manners of Senator McCarthy or the bad judgment of Representative Velde. They have dealt more with the methods of investigators than with the direction of the investigations. With rare exceptions they have done little to expose the dangers inherent in the spread of congressional authority to areas traditionally held to be beyond the reach of legislation. In this large sense the press has defaulted in discharging its censorial function.

Moreover, the press, far from checking congressional investigations, has operated in a vital way to advance their purposes. Without the press, punishment by publicity would have been impossible. When newspapers report the names of individuals called Communists by a senator or by witnesses appearing under a senator's protection, they indelibly stigmatize those individuals as disloyal to their country—and often in the absence of any evidence whatever to substantiate the charges. When legislative trials are turned into journalistic sensations, newspapers play a part in the debasement of due process. They are used, and used deliberately, by congressional investigators as the executioners of sentences arbitrarily imposed—as the beheaders of reputations —and commonly for conduct that the Constitution forbids Congress to declare criminal.

It is often said by critics of the press that the newspapers built up McCarthy and made him a power in the land by keeping his name incessantly in the headlines. There is an element of truth in the stricture, although it leaves out of account the realities of daily journalism. Sensational charges made by a United States senator are news within any meaningful definition of the term; and the public is entitled to know about them and judge them. No responsible newspaper could ignore them or fail to report them simply because it believed them to be untrue. That would be an unwarranted interjection of editorial bias into the news columns. It would be a violation of the objectivity in reporting that every good newspaper tries to achieve.

The tradition of objectivity has lifted the American press from the abusive personal journalism which characterized it seventy-five or one hundred years ago to a level of accuracy and reliability probably unsurpassed by the press of any other country. But the purpose of good reporting must be to give readers a focused picture of the world around them, to keep that picture balanced and proportioned. Elmer Davis once stated the problem in illuminating terms:

The good newspaper, the good news broadcaster, must walk a tightrope between two great gulfs—on one side the false objectivity that takes everything at face value and lets the public be imposed on by the charlatan with the most brazen front; on the other, the "interpretive" reporting which fails to draw the line between objective and subjective, between a reasonably well-established fact and what the reporter or editor wishes were the fact. To say that is easy; to do it is hard. No wonder that too many fall back on the incontrovertible objective fact that the Honorable John P. Hoozis said, colon quote—and never mind whether he was lying or not.[20]

There is, to be sure, no simple formula for the achievement of genuine objectivity. One obviously indispensable ingredient, how-

[20] "News and the Whole Truth," *The Atlantic Monthly*, August 1952, p. 38.

ever, is an unremitting skepticism, a disposition to challenge and probe and scrutinize every handout, every public statement, every accusation. There is nothing in the canons of objectivity that need keep a reporter from asking questions or demanding corroboration. A relentless checking and double-checking are still the roots of good newspaper work. There is nothing in the canons of objectivity that need deprive an accused individual of the presumption of innocence that is his due as a matter of law—and as part of the American tradition. His response deserves the same treatment as the charge against him; and if he has a creditable public record, it deserves to be presented along with the aspersions cast upon it. There is nothing in the canons of objectivity that requires newspapers to treat with even-handed indifference the dredged-up reminiscences of professional witnesses and the denials of their victims.

American newspapers pride themselves on being impervious to the tricks of press agentry. They have learned to detect the contrived publicity release, the planted story, the trial balloon. They do not need to let themselves be used for ulterior purposes by a senatorial highbinder any more than they need to be taken in by a circus press agent or a street-corner pitchman. They do not need to let themselves be sucked in as the purveyors of gossip and, in some cases, of malicious falsehood put out in the guise of news simply because it has been uttered on the floor of Congress or under the auspices of a congressional committee. They may have to report the statements of a demagogue, but they do not have to leave their readers in exclusive reliance on those statements. It is part of their job to put them in perspective. Their aim must be to present not only the truth but the whole truth.

A free press can never be an agency or an instrumentality of the government. Its first responsibility is the guardianship of individual liberty against the tyrannical encroachment of governmental authority. The press in the United States was granted independence of the government precisely to enable it to denounce "with unwearied and even troublesome perseverance" every act of oppression, every needless invasion of individual liberty. Its obligation is to look askance at government. Its duty is to remember what Americans have tended so largely to forget in these days of preoccupation with security—that the eternal vigilance so commonly said to be the price of liberty was meant to be vigilance against duly constituted authority. The role of a free press is to serve, above all else, as the sentinel of freedom.

CHAPTER IX

LEGISLATIVE RESTRAINTS

Congressional investigations in general and senatorial inquisitions in particular are not going to be controlled by the Supreme Court. Let it once for all be understood that the power of inquiry exists, that its possession is a great public trust, and that the American people are going to pour out the vials of their wrath upon those who prove unworthy of the trust. We have evolved worthy standards of conduct for professional baseball players. We are hopeful of a similar evolution in the case of prize fighters. It would be lamentable if only Senators were to be classed as invincibly barbarous.[1]

I

IT IS to Congress itself that the American people have a right to look for the reform and restraint of congressional excesses. Congress is a coordinate and sovereign branch of the United States government and cannot be ruled, though it may be restrained, from the outside. If its manners are to be mended, they must be mended by itself.

Self-control is the most desirable kind of control. There is no need to doubt that the requisite self-control will eventually be found in the United States Congress. It has taken, it is true, a good

[1] Senator George Wharton Pepper, *Family Quarrels* (1931), quoted by George B. Galloway, "Congressional Investigations: Proposed Reforms," *University of Chicago Law Review*, Vol. 18, No. 3 (Spring 1951), p. 495.

deal of extravagance to rouse Congress to a sense of its responsibility in regard to the investigating power. But there are clear signs of a trend toward reform—the clearest of these being, of course, the censure of Senator McCarthy. To doubt that Congress will discipline itself and its investigating committees in the necessary degree is to doubt the whole concept of representative government.

"Every political constitution in which different bodies share the supreme power is only enabled to exist," Lord John Russell once observed, "by the forbearance of those among whom this power is distributed." [2] The possession of power does not always warrant the exercise of it. Latent power has its uses too. And often the test of statesmanship is to leave it latent. This has been, at any rate, part of the genius of the American system. The Executive no less than the legislature has powers which, if abused, could wreck the American Constitution: the power to make war, as distinct from declaring it, the power to proclaim a national emergency and establish martial law, the power to pardon, the power to act as commander-in-chief—all these could be employed arbitrarily if they were not governed by self-discipline and a respect for unwritten codes and great traditions.

The legislative power could be wielded with absolute despotism if it were not held in check every day by a sense of responsibility more powerfully restraining than any of the formal limitations imposed by the Constitution. The power to deny appropriations could be used to nullify the executive branch and eliminate the judicial. "Everybody knows," said Senator George W. Norris in the course of a debate in the Senate in 1938, "that the Constitution says that we shall be the judge of the qualifications of our own Members. If a man came here who was a Democrat, we could say, 'We will not take him in because he is a Democrat.' We could keep him out because of his color or because of his nativity. We could keep him out by reason of his age. We could do any ridiculous or foolish thing we chose to do; but it is

[2] Quoted by Woodrow Wilson, *Congressional Government*, p. 242.

impossible to put together a government on paper without having all those possibilities. If power is to be given to anybody to do anything under a government, it is possible for him to misuse and abuse the power and make it disreputable and destructive." [3]

The very considerable and thoughtful discussion that has taken place in and out of Congress on the need to curb the practices of investigating committees has been focused almost entirely on procedure. But, although procedural reform is important and necessary, it does not really go to the heart of the problem. The basic need is congressional recognition that the investigating power should be kept out of certain areas, even though it can be extended to them legally, and that it should be eschewed for certain purposes, even though the Constitution may not expressly forbid its employment for those purposes. If Congress does not keep its committees from exercising executive functions, from converting hearings into trials, from pushing its authority into areas where no arm of the government should intrude, we shall have a measure of the legislative tyranny against which the Constitutional Convention of 1787 warned and tried to guard.

The investigating power may properly be used—as has been suggested in an earlier portion of this book—for the purpose of informing the Congress on matters about which it contemplates legislation; for the purpose, within limits, of informing the public about emergent national problems; and for the purpose of scrutinizing the performance of executive agencies. It cannot properly be used to "expose" individuals and voluntary associations or to develop evidence for subsequent use in criminal prosecutions. It cannot properly be used to enforce conformity to any official view of what constitutes patriotism or to embarrass heterodoxy and dissent. It cannot properly be used to silence speech or to frustrate lawful association.

[3] *Congressional Record,* March 16, 1938, quoted by Corwin, *The President,* p. 508.

II

Procedural rules can do a great deal to eliminate, or at least minimize, serious infringements of the rights of individuals appearing before investigating bodies. Such rules need not, and should not, impair the effective and proper use of the investigating power in any way. As an indispensable aid to the legislature's work, this power must be kept inviolate for all proper purposes. But there is no necessary conflict between searching and forceful investigation on the one hand and individual rights on the other. The administration of justice is advanced, not impeded, by the obligation of courts to observe procedural rules and standards of due process. The legitimate inquiries of Congress can similarly be strengthened and, incidentally, given an enhanced popular respect, by adherence to principles of fair play.

Perhaps the essential beginning of any set of rules for the conduct of congressional investigations must lie in a recognition that the congressional body which authorizes an investigation is responsible for the manner in which it is carried through. A committee is no more than an agency of the House of Representatives or the Senate; it is wholly without authority on its own account and wields only the power delegated to it by its parent body. This fundamental fact of life about committees has been stated with admirable force by Dean Griswold of the Harvard Law School:

It is wholly clear, I believe, that no Senator or Representative has any power whatever to make an investigation, to require the presence of witnesses and their answers to questions, or to do anything of this sort, merely because he is a Congressman or Senator. An election to the House of Representatives or to the Senate does not make a man any sort of magistrate, nor does it vest him with any power at all over his fellow-citizens except to cast his vote in the body to which he has been elected. The power of investigation is a power which is solely attributable to the collective body, the House of Representatives or the Senate.

Where there is an investigation being conducted, the power that is being exercised is that of the House or the Senate. No committee of either body has any power to conduct any investigation except as a result of a delegation from its House of Congress. No subcommittee of a committee has any power to investigate except on a delegation of the power delegated by the House or Senate to the committee. If there is a subcommittee of one, the power exercised by that one is not any power that is his by virtue merely of his being a member of the legislative body. If he has any power, it is only because there has been a proper delegation or sub-delegation to him of the basic power of the House or Senate.[4]

Thus when Senator McCarthy berates a high officer of the United States Army or browbeats a teacher or a defense-plant worker, he speaks in the name of the Senate, offending its dignity and debasing its prestige. His behavior when he speaks from the floor of the Senate as an individual member is entitled to the tolerance which that body customarily accords the vagaries of its members. The accusations he hurls from public platforms are his own concern, subject only to the statutes against slander and the judgment of his constituents. But when he speaks as the chairman of the Senate's Committee on Government Operations, he speaks with the Senate's voice; witnesses who are contemptuous of him are punishable for contempt not of him or of his committee but of the Senate itself. It is the honor of the Senate which he besmirches if he behaves meanly and vindictively. And this the Senate cannot lightly or carelessly disregard.

Precisely because the House or the Senate is responsible for acts done by committees in its name, these parent bodies have a continuing obligation to survey the practices of committees and to insist upon their adherence to a code of conduct that will not bring their authority into disrepute. The American Bar Association's Special Committee on Individual Rights as Affected by National Security began its recommendations for the reform of investigating procedure with this observation:

The whole history of investigations, confirmed by current examples, shows that it is not enough to create committees and let them proceed as they see fit, often at the whim of the chairman. The scope of their operations should be subjected to continuing congressional scrutiny by

[4] Erwin N. Griswold, Speech at Mount Holyoke College, March 24, 1954.

the whole of the particular House, through a specific group to which is delegated the express duty of supervision of the committees. The day-to-day procedure of the committees should be controlled by a uniform code of procedure which sets a proper standard for all investigations.[5]

The continuing supervision suggested here is an indispensable means of keeping committees responsible and of discharging the responsibility of the House and Senate for their conduct. They have been, until now, laws unto themselves. The real concern of Congress over this situation has been made manifest in the large number and variety of bills which have been proposed to establish uniform procedural rules.

A direct corollary of the need for House and Senate control of committees is the need for committee control of individual members and especially of chairmen. It has been the rule rather than the exception among the special investigating committees—particularly among those engaged in the hunt for subversion—that the chairmen have managed their affairs with absolute autocracy, the other members serving as mere subordinates or supernumeraries. The chairmen have customarily selected the committee staff, determined the topics of inquiry, scheduled the hearings, and decided what witnesses should be subpoenaed; in addition, they have usually spoken for the committee to the press and have exercised their own discretion as to the release of testimony taken in executive session.

Perhaps the most egregious instance of absolutism on the part of a committee chairman was the action of Representative Velde, as chairman of the House Committee on Un-American Activities, in issuing a subpoena to Harry S. Truman without even consulting most of his committee colleagues. This piece of theatricalism occurred in the wake of Attorney General Brownell's sensational charge that the former President had promoted Harry Dexter White, knowing him to have been a Soviet spy. The chairman's action evoked angry protests from the entire Democratic minority of the committee and from some of the Republicans as well. It was, incidentally, a fairly patent violation of the Un-American

[5] Report on Congressional Investigations, August 1954, p. 35.

Activities Committee's own rules, which forbid a "major investigation" to be undertaken without majority approval. Velde's justification for his subpoena to former President Truman was that it did not involve a "major investigation."

Committee responsibility is collective, and committee control ought to be no less so. Basic to any set of rules which Congress may contrive for its committees should be a firm provision for majority rule. And this should apply, as Will Maslow has urged in a distinguished article outlining a model investigating code, to "every important phase of an investigation, including the hiring of staff, the authorization of subsidiary inquiries, the scheduling of hearings, the subpoenaing of witnesses (where policy questions are involved), the release of executive testimony, and the issuance of publications, reports, and public statements." [6]

One of the worst aspects of one-man committee rule has been the holding of one-man hearings, commonly by the chairman acting as a grand inquisitor, sometimes by a committee member permitted, as in the case of Senator Eastland at New Orleans, to serve as a sub-subcommittee. This has resulted sometimes in displays of tyrannical temper, among which Senator McCarthy's abusive treatment of General Zwicker has been only the most publicized instance. The evils inherent in one-man hearings are now pretty generally recognized. Most of the reform proposals forbid them. The Watkins Committee, with the transcript of the Zwicker testimony freshly in mind, added to its recommendations for censure of Senator McCarthy a recommendation that the standing rules of the Senate be amended to provide, among other things, that "no witness shall be required to testify before a committee or subcommittee with less than two members present, unless the committee or subcommittee by majority vote agrees that one member may hold the hearing, or the witness waives any objection to testifying before one member." [7]

A resolution introduced February 24, 1954, by Senator Morse

[6] Will Maslow, "Fair Procedure in Congressional Investigations: A Proposed Code," *Columbia Law Review*, Vol. 54 (June 1954), p. 857.
[7] Report of the Select Committee to Study Censure Charges, p. 67.

and Senator Lehman to establish a Code of Fair Committee Procedure stipulates that "no testimony shall be taken in any hearing unless a majority of the committee is present." [8] The American Bar Association recommends flatly that "the number of members required to conduct the actual hearing should be determined in advance by majority vote. The number so required should be announced to the public. No hearing should be conducted with less than two members present." [9] To this there should certainly be added a proviso that when only two members are sitting they be of different political parties. The interrogation and taking of testimony from a subpoenaed witness is too heady a power to be left in the hands of one man without any restraint from his colleagues. If the requirement that at least two members be present to take testimony imposes some inconvenience on investigators, it is an inconvenience amply warranted by the dangers inherent in one-man interrogations.

Of equal importance with the principle of majority rule is the principle that investigations should be limited to specific subjects and areas clearly defined in the House or Senate resolution establishing the investigating committee. Committees such as the House Committee on Un-American Activities, which make all human endeavor their jurisdiction, are a menace to orderly administration of congressional business and become despotic by their very pretense to omnicompetence. This particular investigating committee, endowed with permanent standing in 1945, has cut across the work of numerous standing committees of the House; its authorization to investigate "the diffusion within the United States of subversive and un-American propaganda"—in the absence of any definition of the key terms—has led it to undertake what would properly be the work of the Judiciary Committee, the Civil Service Committee, the Committee on Education and Labor, even the Foreign Affairs Committee. The same can be said of the roving investigations conducted during the 83rd Congress

[8] *Congressional Record*, February 24, 1954, p. 2098.
[9] Report on Congressional Investigations, p. 37.

by the McCarthy Subcommittee and the Jenner Subcommittee in the Senate.

When the House or Senate delegates its power of investigation to a committee, it ought to do so only for a limited and precisely specified purpose. "The jurisdiction of each investigative committee should be clearly defined," says the report of the American Bar Association. "The resolution is the charter of the committee, and it should state the subject matter and scope of the investigation in such a straightforward fashion that the parent organization, a witness, and counsel for a witness can determine when the committee is exceeding its jurisdiction." [10] Definiteness of this sort is indispensable if a witness and his counsel are to have any reasonable basis for refusing to answer questions they deem improper or irrelevant; and it is indispensable, too, if the parent body is to make a meaningful judgment on the manner in which a committee has discharged its responsibilities.

These twin provisions—majority rule and a definite charter of investigation—are fundamental if investigations are to serve Congress and not merely the whims, ambitions, or vengefulness of individual investigators. There is clear need, in addition, for a procedural code that will guarantee certain rights to witnesses appearing before investigating committees. These rights have been elaborated in a number of proposals offered in and out of Congress. The most important among them are summarized here.

The Right to Fair Notice

Any witness summoned before a congressional investigating committee, and especially a witness called upon to answer serious charges, should have a reasonable opportunity to prepare for the occasion. It is by no means an easy experience for persons unfamiliar with the ways of Congress. Often witnesses have been ordered to appear on no more than a few hours' notice and with no specification of the subject on which they are to be questioned. On one occasion a lawyer, appearing as counsel to a witness be-

[10] Ibid., p. 36.

fore the House Un-American Activities Committee, was himself directed to take the stand forthwith. Subpoenas, or what a committee considers the equivalent of a subpoena, are frequently issued by telegram or telephone. A code of fair procedure ought to provide as a minimum that persons called to testify should be accorded a chance for preparation; this should include at least forty-eight hours' notice and a precise statement of the question under inquiry, so that he may consult counsel, collect his thoughts, and make a considered decision as to his reply. All the proper purposes of an investigating committee will be advanced, not retarded, by observance of this elementary fairness to witnesses.

The Right to Counsel

Nearly all investigating committees permit witnesses to have counsel in attendance when they appear to testify, but the limitations placed upon the counsel's activities make a mockery of this basic right. Usually the counsel can do no more than sit beside his client and give whispered advice when he is asked for it— which is not always when the client needs it most. He cannot volunteer advice or interpose objections to questions he considers improper or cross-examine adverse witnesses; he cannot even examine his client with a view to bringing out testimony he believes to be essential.

These restraints on the right to counsel are imposed on the theory that congressional investigations are not trials and therefore do not require observance of the due process, which would be mandatory in a court; the granting of judicial due process, it has long been argued, would slow up committee proceedings and divert attention from the main point of an investigation. There is certainly substance to this contention. And if, in fact, legislative inquiries never turned into trials, there would be no injustice in abandoning the safeguards courts provide for witnesses. In many committee proceedings testimony is given willingly, and witnesses come before committees, often at their own request, to impart information they want Congress to consider; they are not charged with anything and they have no need to defend themselves. Court-room rules would be a nuisance in such situations.

Sometimes, however—even if committees should become much more careful than they have been in the past to avoid using the investigating power to pass judgment on individuals—witnesses find themselves obliged to answer serious charges of misconduct. When these cases arise—when, in reality, a committee is conducting what amounts to a trial—the delay and inconvenience entailed in the observance of judicial rules ought to be accepted out of respect for the rights of individuals. Observance of these rules would, in point of fact, help a committee to sift conflicting testimony and discover the truth.

A full right to counsel is imperative, both for the sake of the committee and for that of the individual. And this right, if it is to have reality, must include opportunity for counsel to interpose objections, to question the accused and cross-question the accusers. No doubt, as the American Bar Association's Special Committee has suggested, the length of interrogation can be controlled by a majority of the committee in order to prevent abuse. But it must embrace a full chance to present an effective defense. This is no more than to say that if congressional committees are to conduct trials, or what amount to trials, they must be fair trials.

"We have reached such a point in the conducting of Senate investigations which go into the question of the innocence or guilt of persons under investigation," said Senator Morse, "that it is a legal fiction to argue that, in fact, such persons are not standing trial. . . . I am willing to say that there would not be personal liberty for individuals in America if they were deprived of the precious right to be represented by counsel. If a citizen does not have such a right, when he is in a situation which is tantamount to a trial, then he is the victim of an inquisition. Our Founding Fathers recognized that, and, along with other causes of the Revolutionary War, were willing to fight a revolution to bring such a practice to an end." [11]

[11] *Congressional Record*, February 24, 1954, pp. 2098–99.

The feasibility of granting full right to counsel in hearings intended to judge the guilt or innocence of an individual was demonstrated by the Senate itself in the Watkins Committee proceedings on the resolution to censure Senator McCarthy. Here, perhaps because the issue involved a member of the Senate, and also involved the Senate's dignity and honor, counsel for McCarthy was permitted to argue for dismissal of the charges, to examine the defendant, to call and examine witnesses in his behalf, to cross-examine adverse witnesses, and to confer with his client whenever he wished to do so; indeed, the Senate went so far as to provide for public payment of the counsel's fee—a munificence never suggested in the case of witnesses summoned to defend themselves before the McCarthy Subcommittee. This was, admittedly, a most special situation. It is worth noting, however, that the hearings were not inordinately prolonged by this regard for due process. Public confidence in the outcome was greatly enhanced. And, most important of all, McCarthy was afforded a full and fair chance to defend himself. It was worth taking some time and trouble to achieve these ends.

The Right to Reply

Anybody defamed in a congressional hearing ought to be granted a prompt opportunity to defend himself. It has frequently happened that committees have heard testimony gravely reflecting on individuals or organizations, and have issued reports condemning them on the basis of such testimony, without giving them any chance to refute the charges. Sometimes testimony taken in executive session has been made the basis for condemnatory statements by committees, or members of committees, when the target of denunciation did not even know he had been attacked. One simple rule that ought to be rigidly adhered to is that there should be no comment either in a committee report or by any individual member of a committee respecting a person under investigation until that person has been heard in his own defense and the investigation concerning him has been completed.

Executive sessions have some salutary uses for investigating committees. They can be used effectively to test the credibility of witnesses and to sift malicious, misinformed, or patently absurd allegations from those that seem to the committee to have substance or to deserve further study. They can be used to afford accused persons an opportunity to clear up questions without being forced to undergo the embarrassment and injury of a public hearing. They can be used to enable counsel for a committee to plan public hearings so that they will be orderly, concise, and genuinely informative.

They ought never to be used—as they have been used all too frequently—merely to winnow out headline-producing material or to select for humiliation the pleaders of immunity. Most emphatically, they ought never to be used, as Senator McCarthy so flagrantly used them at Fort Monmouth, to leak a disfigured version of the testimony to press and public. If testimony is taken in executive session, there should be a strict prohibition against the disclosure of any portion of it except with the express approval of a majority of the committee; and in this event any person against whom charges have been made should be accorded a fair opportunity for rebuttal, and this rebuttal should be made part of the disclosure.

In addition to these general rules regarding the rights of witnesses, there is one procedural reform that would do a great deal to enhance the prestige and effectiveness of congressional investigations. The meandering, redundant, disordered course so many investigations take is directly traceable to the practice of having questions asked at random by any or every member of the committee. One consequence is that no facet of the inquiry is fully probed; interrogation jumps kaleidoscopically from topic to topic at the whim of the attending members, leaving everybody—press, public, the witness, and the committee itself—in a state of general bewilderment. Another consequence is that the committee members, having behaved as prosecutors, are left with very little capacity to act as judges.

The evils inherent in letting committee members take a direct part in the questioning of witnesses were richly illustrated in the

long television drama of the Army-McCarthy hearings in the late
spring of 1954. The rules of that investigation provided that witnesses might be interrogated in ten-minute salvos, first by counsel
for the investigating subcommittee, then in turn by each of the
subcommittee's seven members, next by counsel for the Army,
and finally by Senator McCarthy as counsel for himself. As soon
as one weary circuit was completed another commenced, each of
the questioners savoring his ten minutes of television time until at
last the questioner and the questioned alike were exhausted. Each
questioner pursued his own pet line of inquiry, and his time ex-
pired almost as soon as his subject had been broached. The procedure, aggravated by McCarthy's practice of interrupting everyone at will on the pretext of raising a point of order, produced
endless repetition and hopeless obfuscation.

The procedure of the Watkins Committee, which in September
1954 investigated the charges contained in the resolution to censure Senator McCarthy, was in almost every important respect
the antithesis of the procedure followed in the Army-McCarthy
hearings. There were, to begin with, no television cameras, no
klieg lights, no photographers' flashbulbs—in short, no circus atmosphere. Strict standards of relevancy were observed in admitting evidence and argument; and Senator Watkins, as chairman
of the committee, sternly forbade and prevented any diversionary
antics by Senator McCarthy.

The Watkins Committee preserved order in an even more significant sense. Its members conducted themselves in the manner of
judges, or at least in the manner of detached hearing examiners.
To a very large extent they simply listened, leaving presentation
of the evidence and interrogation of the witnesses to the committee counsels, E. Wallace Chadwick and Guy G. de Furia, who
had carefully prepared and organized the material to be put
before the committee and the questions to be put to witnesses.
The committee members passed on points of law and upon objections from Senator McCarthy or his counsel; occasionally they
interjected supplementary or clarifying questions of their own.
But they never badgered, harassed, or accused the defendant or

gave any indication of hostility toward him. The result was an atmosphere of calm deliberation, of genuine inquiry.

"The inquiry we are engaged in," said Senator Watkins at the start of the hearings, "is of a special character which differentiates it from the usual legislative inquiry. It involves the internal affairs of the Senate itself in the exercise of a high constitutional function. It is by nature a judicial or semi-judicial function, and we shall attempt to conduct it as such. The procedures outlined are not necessarily appropriate to congressional investigations and should not, therefore, be construed as in any sense intended as a model appropriate to such inquiries. We hope what we are doing will be found to conform to sound senatorial principles and traditions in the special field in which the committee is operating." [12]

Despite Senator Watkins' disclaimer that the procedures followed by his committee were not "in any sense intended as a model," and despite the extraordinary nature of the committee's responsibility, one may reasonably ask why these procedures would not be adaptable in some degree to all inquiries in which a witness is called upon to defend himself against serious charges. The solicitude shown for the rights of a senator ought to be considered appropriate for the rights of any American citizen. If the Senate and the House of Representatives lack the time or the willingness to show such solicitude, then they had better forgo entirely the kind of investigation which entails a judgment of individual guilt or innocence.

III

There is an alternative to the established pattern of congressional investigation that deserves consideration. It lies in delegation of the congressional investigating power, for special purposes and in special situations, not to congressional committees but to fact-finding bodies outside the Senate or the House. No doubt there would be strong resistance in Congress to relinquish-

[12] Report of the Select Committee to Study Censure Charges, p. 4.

ing a function that has yielded such rich dividends in political advancement and renown, but there would be rich dividends on the other side too—in the safeguarding of individual rights, in the release of congressmen from duties that are time-consuming and often tedious, and in the likelihood that more light would be cast on the situation, with much less heat.

In 1928 the Senate, with an eye to easing the burden of investigating committees, went so far as to authorize a delegation of its investigating power. It adopted a resolution providing that "the President of the Senate be, and he hereby is, authorized, on the request of any of the committees of the Senate, to issue commissions to take testimony within the United States or elsewhere." To date, however, this authorization has never been used.

For certain types of investigation it could be extremely useful. Tested models for such delegation can be found in two instrumentalities of the British Parliament—the Royal Commissions and the Tribunals of Inquiry. The Royal Commission is a device for obtaining a thorough and dispassionate survey of some major social problem respecting which legislation may be needed. Composed of eminent men selected as a rule from outside the Parliament, it is able by reason of its detachment from politics and its freedom from other duties to bring to its subject a much more impartial, open-minded, and deliberative approach than could be expected from a legislative committee.

The device has been used several times in the United States, and with an effectiveness that should encourage further recourse to it. The Wickersham Commission, which in 1931 filed a comprehensive report on the entire federal machinery of justice; the Temporary National Economic Committee, which made an exhaustive survey of the nation's economy, resources, and potentials during the second Roosevelt administration; the Hoover Commission, which has been engaged in a continuing study of the organization of the executive branch of the government—all these have made valuable contributions of a kind that no committee of Congress, standing or select, would have had the time, detachment, or facilities to make.

Commissions of this sort could aid Congress immeasurably in assessing such problems, for example, as the effectiveness of the country's internal-security system or the prevalence of interstate gambling and crime. Their reports could inspire much more respect and confidence than those of committees whose members were subject to political pressures and to the suspicion of self-interest. Congress could establish such commissions by joint resolution in situations it deemed appropriate, could carefully prescribe their jurisdiction, and could subject their recommendations to debate, thus keeping its own power unimpaired.

The Tribunals of Inquiry afford a model better suited than the Royal Commission to the special needs of Congress when its investigations involve accusations against individuals. Professor Herman Finer of the University of Chicago has outlined the role of the Tribunals of Inquiry in these terms:

There may be situations in the conduct of government, within it or involved in its outskirts, where considerable doubt prevails about the guilt of persons suspected, so that a charge, for example, under the Official Secrets Acts, or for bribery, or criminal negligence in the supply of instruments or vessels to the government, cannot be exactly formulated or pressed with a proof of criminal intent, having regard to the severity with which the law courts require proof up to the hilt before fastening a conviction on a man. The public may still entertain suspicions. There may still be proof of harm done, short of crime and criminal intent. Behavior may be impure beyond the limits permissible for good democratic government yet short of the limits of criminal action. There may be culpable incompetence or unfaithfulness to trust not yet formulated in the criminal law and perhaps not formulable.

The Tribunal of Inquiry in British law and practice is an attempt to find a procedure that fits such situations—removing a quasi-political misdemeanor from the political arena because the proof should be quasi-judicial, but not taking the case to a law court because the problem is quasi-political. A "political" charge is submitted to the procedure of what is almost a court of law.[13]

There have been but seven such tribunals appointed since the act authorizing them was adopted by Parliament in 1921. They are

[13] Herman Finer, "The British System," *University of Chicago Law Review,* Vol. 18, No. 3 (Spring 1951), p. 562.

usually composed of three members, men of broad experience and the highest repute, often with a judge of the High Court as chairman. Only the concurrence of both Houses of Parliament can authorize creation of a Tribunal of Inquiry, the members of which are then appointed by the Prime Minister and empowered to take evidence on oath, require documents to be produced and witnesses to attend, and conduct hearings appropriate to the subject of its study. Its scope is strictly prescribed in the resolution creating it. In every instance in which they have operated, Tribunals of Inquiry have produced findings which satisfied Parliament and the British public that they had dealt with their subject definitively—and dealt with it fairly and non-politically. There have been few congressional investigations of which so much can be said; a congressional committee starts out under suspicion of political bias.

The idea of a commission of inquiry divorced from the legislature and freed from political partisanship is not an alien one. New York State, through its Moreland Act, fathered by Charles Evans Hughes when he was governor, has been employing such commissions since 1907, with admirable results in terms of efficiency and public confidence. The Moreland Act would no doubt be unsatisfactory to Congress as a model, since it vests the power to create a commission and to appoint its members in the governor. Its report goes to the governor for submission to the legislature. Nevertheless, the New York legislature has maintained the Moreland Act in force for nearly half a century and has reposed the utmost respect in its commissions. Professor Lindsay Rogers of Columbia University says of the act's operation:

Rarely, if ever, has the legislature been able to charge that the governor selected as commissioner a partisan or a nonentity, to criticize the methods of investigation, or to maintain that a report did not carry conviction. Practically all of the commissioners have been men who had reputations that they wished to preserve. . . . Such men were careful to provide themselves with efficient investigators and counsel and did not seek headlines. Their inquiries have ranged over the whole field of New York State's administration. Rarely has the state legislature been hostile to investigations ordered by the governor. . . . If there were a federal Moreland Act, Senators and Representatives might in time be willing to restrain themselves in the same fashion and to wait for a report.[14]

The basic idea of the Moreland Act and of the Tribunals of Inquiry could usefully be adapted to congressional purposes. If Congress preferred to keep control of investigating tribunals entirely in its own hands, it could provide for their creation by concurrent resolution and it could vest the appointing power in the President of the Senate and the Speaker of the House; or, if it allowed the Executive to select the members, it could subject them to senatorial confirmation. Such tribunals would be ideally suited to situations that involved the determination of individual guilt or innocence but that did not warrant criminal indictments and court trials. The tribunals could submit their reports directly to Congress, which would retain the final power to approve or reject them and, when it seemed desirable, to adopt remedial legislation based on their findings.

Tribunals made up of disinterested men of the highest probity and reputation would be of inestimable help to Congress in dealing with problems which congressional committees have neither the time nor the detachment to handle wisely and fairly. They would be instruments of Congress which would preserve for that body all its essential investigating power; but they would eliminate the vice of investigation by committees whose members were at once prosecutors and judges. They would be able to assure an appropriate measure of due process when dealing with the rights and liberties of citizens. Resort to them in special situations would not be a relinquishment of congressional responsibility; it would be an acknowledgment of the responsibility to undertake the solemn business of judgment in an impartial atmosphere.

[14] Lindsay Rogers, "The Problem and Its Solution," *University of Chicago Law Review*, Vol. 18, No. 3 (Spring 1951), pp. 471–72.

IV

When all the rules and codes have been formulated, when all the remedial devices have been adopted, when all the areas of appropriate activity have been defined, the conduct of congressional investigating committees will still depend essentially upon the character of Congress. The conscience of these committees can rise no higher than the conscience of their source.

There will always be McCarthys in a Senate that countenances them. And rules alone will not restrain such men. Senator McCarthy himself has given authoritative testimony on this score. "I don't think you can pass any rule that can make any irresponsible man a responsible man," he said to the Senate Rules Committee at a hearing to consider a code for congressional investigations. In point of fact, the McCarthy Subcommittee's own rules are fairly reasonable and enlightened; the principal trouble with them is that they have never been observed. Nevertheless, procedural rules can be immensely valuable in formulating the criteria by which individual conduct is to be judged.

Perhaps the long and painful self-searching that ended in the censure of McCarthy will do more to reform investigating procedures than any procedural code that can be contrived. For it reflected a sense of honor on the part of the Senate, and a revived regard for that honor. It revealed a recognition, too long suppressed, that the Senate as an institution is the inheritor and the trustee of a great tradition, that its members can never be a law unto themselves but are bound by laws more pressing and compelling than any that can be codified. "The honor of the Senate" may be undefined and undefinable, but it is nonetheless real; and it was essentially for the violation of this honor, rather than for any breach of specific rules, that McCarthy was at last called to account. The Senate's action bespoke an awareness of the moral obligation that inescapably accompanies authority. There is no restraint upon authority so meaningful as the concept of *noblesse oblige.*

The censure of McCarthy gave evidence of the fundamental balance and tough resilience of American democracy, which, in the end, generates its own controls. The excesses of investigating committees were borne for a long time, and with seeming indifference, by both House and Senate—and by the American people—because of a preoccupation with national security and a deep current of national anxiety, which induced a fevered flight from democratic values. There is good reason to hope that this fever has abated. There is good reason to hope for a return to that jealous guardianship of its own good name that animated Congress in the past. In 1929 the Senate did not hesitate to censure one of its members, Hiram Bingham of Connecticut, for an offense which, in the laxity of today's standards, would be considered trivial. This pride of office, this touchy unwillingness to let any member sully the title he bears by virtue of his membership, governs England's Parliament and must again govern its offspring, the Congress of the United States.

Like any other legislative body, the Congress of the United States has had its share of demagogues. But it has also had statesmen capable of rising to great occasions. And, as in the people whom the Congress represents, there are in Congress itself abundant reserves of tolerance, magnanimity, respect for fair play, and faith in its own best traditions. It is in these attributes, in the development of more exacting standards of personal and corporate honor, in the growth of a spirit to which every manifestation of tyranny is abhorrent, that the remedy for abuses of congressional power must be sought. It is in the majesty of Congress that the needed curbs on its conduct will be found.

If Congress has been slow to recognize its responsibility, the forces outside it which have failed to exert the countervailing power expected of them in the American constitutional system must share the blame. The executive branch in recent years has been timorous in resisting legislative encroachments on its jurisdiction. This has been evident in the repeated failure of department and agency chiefs to support subordinates unjustly assailed by congressional investigators; employees known by their superiors to be trustworthy and conscientious have been sacrificed on the altar of political expediency and in the name of "cooperation" with Congress. Cabinet officers have allowed subordinates to be questioned and upbraided about matters of policy instead of going themselves before committees and assuming full responsibility for everything done under their authority; if there is misconduct within a department, it is the head of the department who should be called to account for it and required to correct it or to resign. Executive failure to accept responsibility in this exacting sense has invited congressional attempts to dictate executive action. It has created a vacuum of power into which legislative usurpation has inevitably penetrated.

Still more corrupting, however, has been a failure on the part of the President himself to assert the full power of his tremendous office to counteract the power of the legislative branch. The American system, perhaps more than any other, is dependent on resolute, affirmative executive leadership—leadership which mobilizes public opinion in support of presidential policies and a presidential program. In the absence of such leadership, legislative dominance, and, in the end, legislative tyranny, may prevail. Former President Truman stated this basic fact of American politics with great clarity in an address in New York on May 8, 1954:

The President is responsible for the administration of his office. And that means for the administration of the entire executive branch. It is not the business of Congress to run any of the agencies for him.

Unless this principle is observed, it is impossible to have orderly government. The legislative power will ooze into the executive offices. It will influence and corrupt the decisions of the executive branch. It will affect promotions and transfers. It will warp and twist policies.

Not only does the President cease to be master in his own house, but the whole house of government becomes one which has no master. The power of decision then rests only in the legislative branch, and the legislative branch by its very nature is not equipped to perform these executive functions.

To this kind of encroachment it is the duty of the President to say firmly and flatly "No." The investigative power of Congress is not limitless. It extends only so far as to permit the Congress to acquire the information that it honestly needs to exercise its legislative functions. Exercised beyond those limits, it becomes a manifestation of unconstitutional power. It raises the threat of legislative dictatorship.

The judicial branch, which has not hesitated from time to time to overturn economic legislation enacted by Congress, has been conspicuously slow in imposing any check upon the congressional investigating power when it came into conflict with individual rights. It has not, at any rate, been vigorous in giving freedom of expression and association that preferred place in the American political system to which it has often said they are entitled.

The gravest failure to arrest the overextension of congressional power, however, has been a failure on the part of institutions outside the government to assert and insist upon their independence. The churches, the universities, the foundations, the press, the political action organizations, the professional groups (and most notably the bar associations), even the labor unions and the organized "liberals"—all these have contributed by their complaisance to the development of a dangerous legislative supremacy. They have done little to arouse the American people to a recognition of the perils that such a development conceals.

"We have in this country but one security," said Charles Evans Hughes in a speech at Kingston, N.Y., when he was campaigning for the governorship in 1906. "You may think that the Constitution is your security—it is nothing but a piece of paper. You may think that the statutes are your security—they are nothing but words in a book. You may think that elaborate mechanism of government is your security—it is nothing at all, unless you have sound and uncorrupted public opinion to give life to your Constitution, to give vitality to your statutes, to make efficient your government machinery."

But if the countervailing forces in the American community have been dormant, this is not to say that they cannot be reawakened. They possess latent powers capable of restoring swiftly the equilibrium characteristic of a free society. Against the danger of congressional dominance—against the danger of any manner of tyranny—there is an American genius for adjustment and a rooted respect for individual rights. This is not a nation new to the practice of democracy. It has resources, when occasion quickens them, to produce the kind of interplay that will re-establish the balanced unity of the Constitution.

INDEX

INDEX